George John Romanes

A Candid Examination of Theism

George John Romanes

A Candid Examination of Theism

ISBN/EAN: 9783743382510

Manufactured in Europe, USA, Canada, Australia, Japa

Cover: Foto ©Thomas Meinert / pixelio.de

Manufactured and distributed by brebook publishing software (www.brebook.com)

George John Romanes

A Candid Examination of Theism

A CANDID EXAMINATION

OF

THEISM.

BY

PHYSICUS.

LONDON:
TRÜBNER & CO., LUDGATE HILL.
1878.
[*All rights reserved.*]

CANST THOU BY SEARCHING FIND OUT GOD?

PREFACE.

THE following essay was written several years ago; but I have hitherto refrained from publishing it, lest, after having done so, I should find that more mature thought had modified the conclusions which the essay sets forth. Judging, however, that it is now more than ever improbable that I shall myself be able to detect any errors in my reasoning, I feel that it is time to present the latter to the contemplation of other minds; and in doing so, I make this explanation only because I feel it desirable to state at the outset that the present treatise was written before the publication of Mr. Mill's treatise on the same subject. It is desirable to make this statement, first, because in several instances the trains of reasoning in the two essays are parallel, and next, because in other instances I have quoted passages from Mr. Mill's essay in connections which would be scarcely intelligible were it not understood that these passages are insertions made after the present essay had been completed. I have also added several supplementary essays which have been written since the main essay was finished.

It is desirable further to observe, that the only reason why I publish this edition anonymously is because I feel very strongly that, in matters of the kind with which the present essay deals, opinions and arguments should be allowed to produce the exact degree of influence to which as opinions and arguments they are entitled: they should be permitted to stand upon their own intrinsic merits alone, and quite beyond the shadow of that unfair pre-judication which cannot but arise so soon as their author's authority, or absence of authority, becomes known. Notwithstanding this avowal, however, I fear that many who glance over the following pages will read in the "Physicus" of the first one a very different motive. There is at the present time a wonderfully wide-spread sentiment pervading all classes of society—a sentiment which it would not be easy to define, but the practical outcome of which is, that to discuss the question of which this essay treats is, in some way or other, morally wrong. Many, therefore, who share this sentiment will doubtless attribute my reticence to a puerile fear on my part to meet it. I can only say that such is not the case. Although I allude to this sentiment with all respect—believing as I do that it is an offshoot from the stock which contains all that is best and greatest in human nature—nevertheless it seems to me impossible to deny that the sentiment in question is as unreasonable as the frame of mind which harbours it must be un-reasoning. If there is no God, where can be the harm in our examining the spurious evidence of his existence? If there is a God, surely our first duty towards him must be to exert to our utmost, in our attempts to find him, the most noble faculty with which he has endowed us—as carefully to investigate the evidence which he has seen fit to furnish of his own existence as we investigate the evidence of inferior things in his dependent creation. To say that there is one rule or method for ascertaining truth in the latter case, which it is not legitimate to apply in the former case, is merely a covert way of saying that the Deity, if he exists, has not supplied us with rational evidence of his existence. For my own part, I feel that such an assertion cannot but embody far more unworthy conceptions of a Personal God than are represented by any amount of earnest inquiry into whatever evidence of his existence there may be present; but, neglecting this reflection, if there is a God, it is certain that reason is the faculty by which he has enabled man to discover truth, and it is no less certain that the scientific methods have proved themselves by far the most trustworthy for reason to adopt. To my mind, therefore, it is impossible to resist the conclusion that, looking to this undoubted pre-eminence of the scientific methods as ways to truth, whether or not there is a God, the question as to his existence is both more morally and more reverently contemplated if we regard it purely as a problem for methodical analysis to solve, than if we regard it in any other light. Or, stating the case in other words, I believe that in whatever degree we intentionally abstain from using in this case what we *know* to be the most trustworthy methods of inquiry in other cases, in that degree are we either unworthily closing our eyes to a dreaded truth, or we are guilty of the worst among human sins—" Depart from us, for we desire not the knowledge of thy ways." If it is said that, supposing man to be in a state of probation, faith, and not reason, must be the instrument of his trial, I am ready to admit the validity of the remark; but I must also ask it to be remembered, that unless faith has *some* basis of reason whereon to rest, it differs in nothing from superstition; and hence that it is still our duty to investigate the *rational* standing of the question before us by the *scientific* methods alone. And I may here observe parenthetically, that the same reasoning applies to all investigations concerning the reality of a supposed revelation. With such investigations, however, the present essay has nothing to do, although I may remark that if there is any evidence of a Divine Mind discernible in the structure of a professing revelation, such evidence, in whatever degree present, would be of the best possible kind for substantiating the hypothesis of Theism.

Such being, then, what I conceive the only reasonable, as well as the most truly moral, way of regarding the question to be discussed in the following pages, even if the conclusions yielded by this discussion were more negative than they are, I should deem it culpable cowardice in me *for this reason* to publish anonymously. For even if an inquiry of the present kind could ever result in a final demonstration of Atheism, there might be much for its author to regret, but nothing for him to be ashamed of; and, by parity of reasoning, in whatever degree the result of such an inquiry is seen to have a tendency to negative the theistic theory, the author should not be ashamed candidly to acknowledge his conviction as to the degree of such tendency, provided only that his conviction is an *honest* one, and that he is conscious of its having been reached by using his faculties with the utmost care of which he is capable.

If it is retorted that the question to be dealt with is of so ultimate a character that even the scientific methods are here untrustworthy, I reply that they are nevertheless the *best* methods available, and hence that the retort is without pertinence: the question is still to be regarded as a scientific one, although we may perceive that neither an affirmative nor a negative answer can be given to it with any approach to a full demonstration. But if the question is thus conceded to be one falling within the legitimate scope of rational inquiry, it follows that the mere fact of demonstrative certainty being here antecedently impossible should not deter us from instituting the inquiry. It is a well-recognised principle of scientific research, that however difficult or impossible it may be to *prove* a given theory true or false, the theory should nevertheless be tested, so far as it admits of being tested, by the full rigour of the scientific methods. Where demonstration cannot be hoped for, it still remains desirable to reduce the question at issue to the last analysis of which it is capable.

Adopting these principles, therefore, I have endeavoured in the following analysis to fix the precise standing of the evidence in favour of the theory of Theism, when the latter is viewed in all the flood of light which the progress of modern science—physical and speculative—has shed upon it. And forasmuch as it is impossible that demonstrated truth can ever be shown untrue, and forasmuch as the demonstrated truths on which the present examination rests are the most fundamental which it is possible for the human mind to reach, I do not think it presumptuous to assert what appears to me a necessary deduction from these facts—namely, that, possible errors in reasoning apart, the rational position of Theism as here defined must remain without material modification as long as our intelligence remains human.

LONDON, 1878.

ANALYSIS.

CHAPTER I.

EXAMINATION OF ILLOGICAL ARGUMENTS IN FAVOUR OF THEISM.

SECT.		PAGE
1.	Introductory	1
2.	Object of the chapter	2
3.	The Argument from the Inconceivability of Self-existence .	2
4.	The Argument from the Desirability of there being a God .	3
5.	The Argument from the Presence of Human Aspirations .	3
6.	The Argument from Consciousness	4
7.	The Argument for a First Cause	6

CHAPTER II.

THE ARGUMENT FROM THE EXISTENCE OF THE HUMAN MIND.

8. Introductory 10
9. Examination of the Argument, and the independent coincidence of my views regarding it with those of Mr. Mill . 10
10. Locke's exposition of the Argument, and a re-enunciation of it in the form of a Syllogism 11
11. The Syllogism defective in that it cannot explain Mind in the abstract. Mill quoted and answered. This defect in the Syllogism clearly defined 12
12. The Syllogism further defective, in that it assumes Intelligence to be the only possible cause of Intelligence. This assumption amounts to begging the whole question as to the being of a God. Inconceivability of Matter thinking

SECT.		PAGE
	no proof that it may not think. Locke himself strangely concedes this. His fallacies and self-contradictions pointed out in an Appendix	14
13.	Objector to the Syllogism need not be a Materialist, but assuming that he is one, he is as much entitled to the hypothesis that Matter thinks as a Theist is to his hypothesis that it does not	16
14.	The two hypotheses are thus of exactly equivalent value, save that while Theism is arbitrary, Materialism has a certain basis of fact to rest upon. This basis defined in a footnote, where also Professor Clifford's essay on "Body and Mind" is briefly examined. Difficulty of estimating the worth of the Argument as to the *most* conceivable being *most* likely true	17
15.	Locke's comparison between certainty of the Inconceivability Argument as applied to Theism and to mathematics shown to contain a *virtual* though not a *formal* fallacy	19
16.	Summary of considerations as to the value of this Argument from Inconceivability	20
17.	Introductory to the other Arguments in favour of the conclusion that only Intelligence can have caused Intelligence	21
18.	Locke's presentation of the view that the cause must contain all that is contained in the effects. His statements contradicted. Mill quoted to show that the analogy of Nature is against the doctrine of higher perfections never growing out of lower ones	21
19.	Enunciation of the last of the Arguments in favour of the proposition that only Intelligence can cause Intelligence. Hamilton quoted to show that in his philosophy the entire question as to the being of a God hinges upon that as to whether or not human volitions are caused . .	22
20.	Absurdity of the old theory of Free-will. Hamilton erroneously identified this theory with the fact that we possess a moral sense. His resulting dilemma . .	23
21.	Although Hamilton was wrong in thus identifying genuine fact with spurious theory, yet his Argument from the fact of our having a moral sense remains to be considered .	26
22.	The question here is merely as to whether or not the presence of the moral sense can be explained by natural causes. *A priori* probability of the moral sense having been evolved. *A posteriori* confirmation supplied by Utilitarianism, &c.	27

CHAPTER III.

THE ARGUMENT FROM DESIGN.

SECT.		PAGE
23.	Mill's presentation of the Argument a resuscitation of Paley's. His criticism on Paley shown to be unfair	36
24.	The real fallacy of Paley's presentation pointed out	37
25.	The same fallacy pointed out in another way	38
26.	Paley's typical case quoted and examined, in order to illustrate the root-fallacy of his Argument from Design. Mill's observations upon this Argument criticised	40
27.	Result yielded by the present analysis of the Argument from Design. The Argument shown to be a *petitio principii*	43

CHAPTER IV.

THE ARGUMENT FROM GENERAL LAWS.

28.	My belief that no competent writer in favour of the Argument from Design could have written upon it at all, had it not been for his instinctive appreciation of the much more important Argument from General Laws. The nature of this Argument stated, and its cogency insisted upon	45
29.	The rational standing of the Argument from General Laws prior to the enunciation of the doctrine of the Conservation of Energy. The Rev. Baden Powell quoted	47
30.	The nature of General Laws when these are interpreted in terms of the doctrine of the Conservation of Energy. The word "Law" defined in terms of this doctrine	52
31.	The rational standing of the Argument from General Laws subsequent to the enunciation of the doctrine of the Conservation of Energy	53
32.	The self-evolution of General Laws, or the objective aspect of the question as to whether we may infer the presence of Mind in Nature because Nature admits of being intelligently interrogated	54
33.	The subjective aspect of this question, according to the data afforded by evolutionary psychology	57

CONTENTS.

SECT.   PAGE

34. Correspondence between products due to human intelligence and products supposed due to Divine Intelligence, a correspondence which is only generic. Illustrations drawn from prodigality in Nature. Further illustrations. Illogical manner in which natural theologians deal with such difficulties. The generic resemblance contemplated is just what we should expect to find, if the doctrine of evolutionary psychology be true 60
35. The last three sections parenthetical. Necessary nature of the conclusion which follows from the last five sections . 63

CHAPTER V.

THE LOGICAL STANDING OF THE QUESTION AS TO THE BEING OF A GOD.

36. Emphatic re-statement of the conclusion reached in the previous chapter. This conclusion shown to be of merely scientific, and not of logical conclusiveness. Preparation for considering the question in its purely logical form . 64
37. The logic of probability in general explained, and canon of interpretation enunciated 66
38. Application of this canon to the particular case of Theism 67
39. Exposition of the logical state of the question . . . 67
40. Exposition continued 69
41. Result of the exposition; "Suspended Judgment" the only logical attitude of mind with regard to the question of Theism 70

CHAPTER VI.

THE ARGUMENT FROM METAPHYSICAL TELEOLOGY.

42. Statement of the position to which the question of Theism has been reduced by the foregoing analysis . . . 72
43. Distinction between a scientific and a metaphysical teleology. Statement of the latter in legitimate terms. Criticism of this statement legitimately made on the side of Atheism as being gratuitous. Impartial judgment on this criticism 74

SECT.		PAGE
44.	Examination of the question as to whether the metaphysical system of teleology is really destitute of all rational support. Pleading of a supposed Theist in support of the system. The principle of correlation of general laws. The complexity of Nature . . .	78
45.	Summary of the Theist's pleading, and judgment that it fairly removes from the hypothesis of metaphysical teleology the charge of the latter being gratuitous .	80
46.	Examination of the degree of probability that is presented by the hypothesis of metaphysical teleology, comprising an examination of the Theistic objection to the scientific train of reasoning on account of its symbolism, and showing that a no less cogent objection lies against the metaphysical train of reasoning on account of its embodying the supposition of unknowable causes. Distinction between "inconceivability" in a formal or symbolical, and in a material or realisable sense. Reply of a supposed Atheist to the previous pleading of the supposed Theist. Herbert Spencer quoted on inconceivability of cosmic evolution as due to Mind . . .	83
47.	Final judgment on the rational value of a metaphysical system of teleology. Distinction between "inconceivability" in an absolute and in a relative sense. Final judgment on the attitude of mind which it is rational to adopt towards the question of Theism. The desirability and the rationality of tolerance in this particular case .	93

CHAPTER VII.

GENERAL SUMMARY AND CONCLUSIONS.

48.	General summary of the whole essay	102
49.	Concluding remarks	110

APPENDIX AND SUPPLEMENTARY ESSAYS.

APPENDIX.

    A Critical Exposition of a Fallacy in Locke's use of the Argument against the possibility of Matter thinking on grounds of its being inconceivable that it should . . 117

SUPPLEMENTARY ESSAY I.
    Examination of Mr. Herbert Spencer's Theistical Argument, and criticism to show that it is inadequate to sustain the doctrine of "Cosmic Theism" which Mr. Fiske endeavours to rear upon it 129

SUPPLEMENTARY ESSAY II.
    A Critical Examination of the Rev. Professor Flint's work on "Theism" 152

SUPPLEMENTARY ESSAY III.
    On the Speculative Standing of Materialism . . . 181

SUPPLEMENTARY ESSAY IV.
    On the Final Mystery of Things 189

THEISM.

CHAPTER I.

EXAMINATION OF ILLOGICAL ARGUMENTS IN FAVOUR OF THEISM.

§ 1. FEW subjects have occupied so much attention among speculative thinkers as that which relates to the being of God. Notwithstanding, however, the great amount that has been written on this subject, I am not aware that any one has successfully endeavoured to approach it, on all its various sides, from the ground of pure reason alone, and thus to fix, as nearly as possible, the exact position which, in pure reason, this subject ought to occupy. Perhaps it will be thought that an exception to this statement ought to be made in favour of John Stuart Mill's posthumous essay on Theism; but from my great respect for this author, I should rather be inclined to regard that essay as a criticism on illogical arguments, than as a *careful* or *matured* attempt to formulate the strictly rational *status* of the question in all its bearings. Nevertheless, as this essay is in some respects the most scientific, just, and cogent, which has yet appeared on the subject of which it treats, and as anything which came from the pen of that great and accurate thinker is deserving of the most serious attention, I shall carefully consider his views throughout the course of the following pages.

Seeing then that, with this partial exception, no competent writer has hitherto endeavoured once for all to settle the long-standing question as to the rational probability of Theism, I cannot but feel that any attempt, however imperfect, to do this, will be welcome to thinkers of every school—the more so in view of the fact that the prodigious rapidity which of late years has marked the advance both of physical and of speculative science, has afforded highly valuable data for assisting us towards a reasonable and, I think, a final decision as to the strictly logical standing of this important matter. However, be my attempt welcome or no, I feel that it is my obvious duty to publish the results which have been yielded by an honest and careful analysis.

§ 2. I may most fitly begin this analysis by briefly disposing of such arguments in favour of Theism as are manifestly erroneous. And I do this the more willingly because, as these arguments are at the present time most in vogue, an exposure of their fallacies may perhaps deter our popular apologists of the future from drawing upon themselves the silent contempt of every reader whose intellect is not either prejudiced or imbecile.

§ 3. A favourite piece of apologetic juggling is that of first demolishing Atheism, Pantheism, Materialism, &c., by successively calling upon them to explain the mystery of self-existence, and then tacitly assuming that the need of such an explanation is absent in the case of Theism—as though the attribute in question were more conceivable when posited in a Deity than when posited elsewhere.

It is, I hope, unnecessary to observe that, so far as the ultimate mystery of existence is concerned, any and every theory of things is equally entitled to the inexplicable fact that something is; and that any endeavour on the part of the votaries of one theory to shift from themselves to the votaries of another theory the *onus* of explaining the necessarily inexplicable, is an instance of irrationality which borders on the ludicrous.

§ 4. Another argument, or semblance of an argument, is the very prevalent one, "Our heart requires a God; therefore it is probable that there is a God:" as though such a subjective necessity, even if made out, could ever prove an objective existence.[1]

§ 5. If it is said that the theistic aspirations of the human heart, by the mere fact of their presence, point to the existence of a God as to their explanatory cause, I answer that the argument would only be valid after the possibility of any more proximate causes having been in action has been excluded—else the theistic explanation violates the fundamental rule of science, the Law of Parcimony, or the law which forbids us to assume the action of more remote causes where more proximate ones are found sufficient to explain the effects. Consequently, the validity of the argument now under consideration is inversely proportional to the number of possibilities there are of the aspirations in question being due to the agency of physical causes; and forasmuch as our ignorance of psychological causation is well-nigh total, the Law of Parcimony forbids us to allow any determinate degree of logical value to the present argument. In other

---

[1] The above was written before Mr. Mill's essay on Theism was published. Lest, therefore, my refutation may be deemed too curt, I supplement it with Mr. Mill's remarks upon the same subject. "It may still be maintained that the feelings of morality make the existence of God eminently desirable. No doubt they do, and that is the great reason why we find that good men and women cling to the belief, and are pained by its being questioned. But, surely, it is not legitimate to assume that, in the order of the universe, whatever is desirable is true. Optimism, even when a God is already believed in, is a thorny doctrine to maintain, and had to be taken by Leibnitz in the limited sense, that the universe being made by a good being, is the best universe possible, not the best absolutely: that the Divine power, in short, was not equal to making it more free from imperfections than it is. But optimism, prior to belief in a God, and as the ground of that belief, seems one of the oddest of all speculative delusions. Nothing, however, I believe, contributes more to keep up the belief in the general mind of humanity than the feeling of its desirableness, which, when clothed, as it very often is, in the form of an argument, is a *naive* expression of the tendency of the human mind to believe whatever is agreeable to it. Positive value the argument of course has none." For Mill's remarks on the version of the argument dealt with in § 5, see his "Three Essays," p. 204.

words, we must not use the absence of knowledge as equivolent to its presence—must not argue from our ignorance of psychological possibilities, as though this ignorance were knowledge of corresponding impossibilities. The burden of proof thus lies on the side of Theism, and from the nature of the case this burden cannot be discharged until the science of psychology shall have been fully perfected. I may add that, for my own part, I cannot help feeling that, even in the present embryonic condition of this science, we are not without some indications of the manner in which the aspirations in question arose; but even were this not so, the above considerations prove that the argument before us is invalid. If it is retorted that the fact of these aspirations having had *proximate* causes to account for their origin, even if made out, would not negative the inference of these being due to a Deity as to their *ultimate* cause; I answer that this is not to use the argument from the presence of these aspirations; it is merely to beg the question as to the being of a God.

§ 6. Next, we may consider the argument from consciousness. Many persons ground their belief in the existence of a Deity upon a real or supposed necessity of their own subjective thought. I say "real or supposed," because, in its bearing upon rational argument, it is of no consequence of which character the alleged necessity actually is. Even if the necessity of thought be real, all that the fact entitles the thinker to affirm is, that it is impossible for *him*, by any effort of thinking, to rid himself of the persuasion that God exists; he is not entitled to affirm that this persuasion is necessarily bound up with the constitution of the human mind. Or, as Mill puts it, "One man cannot by proclaiming with ever so much confidence that *he* perceives an object, convince other people that they see it too. . . . When no claim is set up to any peculiar gift, but we are told that all of us are as capable of seeing what he sees, feeling what he feels, nay, that we actually do so, and when the utmost effort of which we are capable fails to make us aware of what we are told, we perceive this supposed universal faculty of intuition is but

> ' The Dark Lantern of the Spirit
> Which none see by but those who bear it.' "

It is thus, I think, abundantly certain that the present argument must, from its very nature, be powerless as an argument to anyone save its assertor; as a matter of fact, the alleged necessity of thought is not universal; it is peculiar to those who employ the argument.

And now, it is but just to go one step further and to question whether the alleged necessity of thought is, in any case and properly speaking, a *real* necessity. Unless those who advance the present argument are the victims of some mental aberration, it is overwhelmingly improbable that their minds should differ in a fundamental and important attribute from the minds of the vast majority of their species. Or, to continue the above quotation, "They may fairly be asked to consider, whether it is not more likely that they are mistaken as to the origin of an impression in their minds, than that others are ignorant of the very existence of an impression in theirs." No doubt it is true that education and habits of thought may so stereotype the intellectual faculties, that at last what is conceivable to one man or generation may not be so to another;[1] but to adduce this consideration in this place would clearly be but to destroy the argument from the *intuitive* necessity of believing in a God.

Lastly, although superfluous, it may be well to point out that even if the impossibility of conceiving the negation of God were an universal law of human mind—which it certainly is not—the fact of his existence could not be thus proved. Doubtless it would be felt to be much more probable than it now is—as probable, for

---

[1] The words "or not conceivable," are here used in the sense of "not relatively conceivable," as explained in Chap. vi.

instance, if not more probable, than is the existence of an external world;—but still it would not be necessarily true.

§ 7. The argument from the general consent of mankind is so clearly fallacious, both as to facts and principles, that I shall pass it over and proceed at once to the last of the untenable arguments—that, namely, from the existence of a First Cause. And here I should like to express myself indebted to Mr. Mill for the following ideas:—
"The cause of every change is a prior change; and such it cannot but be; for if there were no new antecedent, there would be no new consequent. If the state of facts which brings the phenomenon into existence, had existed always or for an indefinite duration, the effect also would have existed always or been produced an indefinite time ago. It is thus a necessary part of the fact of causation, within the sphere of experience, that the causes as well as the effects had a beginning in time, and were themselves caused. It would seem, therefore, that our experience, instead of furnishing an argument for a first cause, is repugnant to it; and that the very essence of causation, as it exists within the limits of our knowledge, is incompatible with a First Cause."

The rest of Mr. Mill's remarks upon the First Cause argument are tolerably obvious, and had occurred to me before the publication of his essay. I shall, however, adhere to his order of presenting them.

"But it is necessary to look more particularly into this matter, and analyse more closely the nature of the causes of which mankind have experience. For if it should turn out that though all causes have a beginning, there is in all of them a permanent element which had no beginning, this permanent element may with some justice be termed a first or universal cause, inasmuch as though not sufficient of itself to cause anything, it enters as a con-cause into all causation."

He then shows that the doctrine of the Conservation

of Energy supplies us with such a datum, and thus the conclusion easily follows—" It would seem, then, that the only sense in which experience supports, in any shape, the doctrine of a First Cause, viz., as the primæval and universal element of all causes, the First Cause can be no other than Force."

Still, however, it may be maintained that "all force is will-force." But "if there be any truth in the doctrine of Conservation of Force, . . . this doctrine does not change from true to false when it reaches the field of voluntary agency. The will does not, any more than other agencies, create Force: granting that it originates motion, it has no means of doing so but by converting into that particular manifestation, a portion of Force which already existed in other forms. It is known that the source from which this portion of Force is derived, is chiefly, or entirely, the force evolved in the processes of chemical composition and decomposition which constitute the body of nutrition: the force so liberated becomes a fund upon which every muscular and every nervous action, as of a train of thought, is a draft. It is in this sense only that, according to the best lights of science, volition is an originating cause. Volition, therefore, does not answer to the idea of a First Cause; since Force must, in every instance, be assumed as prior to it; and there is not the slightest colour, derived from experience, for supposing Force itself to have been created by a volition. As far as anything can be concluded from human experience, Force has all the attributes of a thing eternal and uncreated. . . .

" All that can be affirmed (even) by the strongest assertion of the Freedom of the Will, is that volitions are themselves uncaused and are, therefore, alone fit to be the first or universal cause. But, even assuming volitions to be uncaused, the properties of matter, so far as experience discloses, are uncaused also, and have the advantage over any particular volition, in being, so far as experience can show, eternal. Theism, therefore, in so far as it rests on the necessity of a First Cause, has no support from experience."

Such may be taken as a sufficient refutation of the argument that, as human volition is apparently a cause in nature, and moreover constitutes the basis of our conception of all causation, therefore all causation is probably volitional in character. But as this is a favourite argument with some theists, I shall introduce another quotation from Mr. Mill, which is taken from a different work.

"Volitions are not known to produce anything directly except nervous action, for the will influences even the muscles only through the nerves. Though it were granted, then, that every phenomenon has an efficient and not merely a phenomenal cause, and that volition, in the case of the particular phenomena which are known to be produced by it, is that cause; are we therefore to say with these writers that since we know of no other efficient cause, and ought not to assume one without evidence, there *is* no other, and volition is the direct cause of all phenomena? A more outrageous stretch of inference could hardly be made. Because among the infinite variety of the phenomena of nature there is one, namely, a particular mode of action of certain nerves which has for its cause and, as we are now supposing, for its efficient cause, a state of our mind; and because this is the only efficient cause of which we are conscious, being the only one of which, in the nature of the case, we *can* be conscious, since it is the only one which exists within ourselves; does this justify us in concluding that all other phenomena must have the same kind of efficient cause with that one eminently special, narrow, and peculiarly human or animal phenomenon?" It is then shown that a logical parallel to this mode of inference is that of generalising from the one known instance of the earth being inhabited, to the conclusion that "every heavenly body without exception, sun, planet, satellite, comet, fixed star, or nebula, is inhabited, and must be so from the inherent constitution of things." After which the passage continues, "It is true there are cases in which, with acknowledged propriety, we generalise from a single instance to a multitude of instances. But they must be instances which resemble the one known instance, and not such as have no circumstance in common with it except that of being instances. . . . But the supporters of the volition theory ask us to infer that volition causes everything, for no other reason except that it causes one particular thing; although that one phenomenon, far from being a type of all natural phenomena, is eminently peculiar; its laws bearing scarcely any resemblance to those of any other phenomenon, whether of inorganic or of organic nature."[1]

[1] For the full discussion from which the above is an extract, see *System of Logic*, vol. i. pp. 409-426 (8th ed.). But, substituting "psychical" for "volitional," see also, for some mitigation of the severity of the above statement, the closing paragraphs of my supplementary essay on "Cosmic Theism."

CHAPTER II.

THE ARGUMENT FROM THE EXISTENCE OF THE HUMAN MIND.

§ 8. LEAVING now the obviously untenable arguments, we next come to those which, in my opinion, may properly be termed scientific.

It will be convenient to classify these as three in number; and under one or other of these heads nearly all the more intelligent advocates of Theism will be found to range themselves.

§ 9. We have first the argument drawn from the existence of the human mind. This is an argument which, for at least the last three centuries, and especially during the present one, has been more relied upon than any other by philosophical thinkers. It consists in the reflection that the being of our own subjective intelligence is the most certain fact which our experience supplies, that this fact demands an adequate cause for its explanation, and that the only adequate cause of our intelligence must be some other intelligence. Granting the existence of a conditioned intelligence (and no one could reasonably suppose his own intelligence to be otherwise), and the existence of an unconditioned intelligence becomes a logical necessity, unless we deny either the validity of the principle that every effect must have an adequate cause, or else that the only adequate cause of Mind is Mind.

It has been a great satisfaction to me to find that my examination of this argument—an examination which was undertaken and completed several months before Mr.

Mill's essay apppeared—has been minutely corroborated by that of our great logician. I mention this circumstance here, as on previous occasions, not for the petty motive of vindicating my own originality, but because in matters of this kind the accuracy of the reasoning employed, and therefore the logical validity of the conclusions attained, are guaranteed in the best possible manner, if the trains of thought have been independently pursued by different minds.

§ 10. Seeing that, among the advocates of this argument, Locke went so far as to maintain that by it alone he could render the existence of a Deity as certain as any mathematical demonstration, it is only fair, preparatory to our examining this argument, to present it in the words of this great thinker.

He says:—"There was a time when there was no knowing (*i.e.*, conscious) being, and when knowledge began to be; or else there has been also a knowing being from all eternity. If it be said, there was a time when no being had any knowledge, when that eternal being was void of all understanding, I reply, that then it was impossible there should ever have been any knowledge: it being as impossible that things wholly void of knowledge, and operating blindly, and without perception, should produce a knowing being, as it is impossible that a triangle should make itself three angles bigger than two right ones. For it is as repugnant to the idea of senseless matter, that it should put into itself, sense, perception, and knowledge, as it is repugnant to the idea of a triangle, that it should put into itself greater angles than two right ones." [1]

Now, although this argument has been more fully elaborate by other writers, the above presentation contains its whole essence. It will be seen that it has the great advantage of resting *immediately* upon the foundation from which all argument concerning this or any other

[1] Essay on Understanding—Existence of God.

matter, must necessarily arise, viz.,—upon the very existence of our argumentative faculty itself. For the sake of a critical examination, it is desirable to throw the argument before us into the syllogistic form. It will then stand thus:—

All known minds are caused by an unknown mind. Our mind is a known mind; therefore, our mind is caused by an unknown mind.

Now the major premiss of this syllogism is inadmissible for two reasons: in the first place, it is assumed that known mind can only be caused by unknown mind; and, in the second place, even if this assumption were granted, it would not explain the existence of Mind as Mind. To take the last of these objections first, in the words of Mr. Mill, "If the mere existence of Mind is supposed to require, as a necessary antecedent, another Mind greater and more powerful, the difficulty is not removed by going one step back: the creating mind stands as much in need of another mind to be the source of its existence as the created mind. Be it remembered that we have no direct knowledge (at least apart from Revelation) of a mind which is even apparently eternal, as Force and Matter are: an eternal mind is, as far as the present argument is concerned, a simple hypothesis to account for the minds which we know to exist. Now it is essential to an hypothesis that, if admitted, it should at least remove the difficulty and account for the facts. But it does not account for mind to refer our mind to a prior mind for its origin. The problem remains unsolved, nay, rather increased."

Nevertheless, I think that it is open to a Theist to answer, "My object is not to explain the existence of Mind in the abstract, any more than it is my object to explain Existence itself in the abstract—to either of which absurd attempts Mr. Mill's reasoning would be equally applicable;—but I seek for an explanation of *my own individual finite mind*, which I know to have had a beginning in time, and which, therefore, in accordance with the widest and most complete analogy that experience supplies, I believe to have been *caused*. And if there is no other objection to my believing in Intelligence as the cause of my intelligence, than that I cannot prove my own intelligence caused, then I am satisfied to let the matter rest here; for as every argument must have *some* basis of assumption to stand upon, I am well pleased to find that the basis in this case is the most solid which experience can supply, viz.,—the law of causation. Fully admitting that it does not account for Mind (in the abstract) to refer one mind to a prior mind for its origin; yet my hypothesis, if admitted, *does* account for the fact that *my mind* exists; and this is all that my hypothesis is intended to cover. For to endeavour to *explain* the existence of an *eternal* mind, could only be done by those who do not understand the meaning of these words."

Now, I think that this reply to Mr. Mill, on the part of a theist, would so far be legitimate; the theistic hypothesis *does* supply a provisional explanation of the existence of known minds, and it is, therefore, an explanation which, in lieu of a better, a theist may be allowed to retain. But a theist may not be allowed to confuse this provisional explanation of his own mind's existence with that of the existence of Mind in the abstract; he must not be allowed to suppose that, by thus hypothetically explaining the existence of known minds, he is thereby establishing a probability in favour of that hypothetical cause, an Unknown Mind. Only if he has some independent reason to infer that such an Unknown Mind exists, could such a probability be made out, and his hypothetical explanation of known mind become of more value than a guess. In other words, although the theistic hypothesis supplies *a possible* explanation of known mind, we have no reason to conclude that it is *the true* explanation, unless other reasons can be shown to justify, on independent grounds, the validity of the theistic hypothesis.

Hence it is manifestly absurd to adduce this explanation as evidence of the hypothesis on which it rests—to argue that Theism must therefore be true, because we assume it to be so, in order to explain *known* mind, as distinguished from *Mind*. If it be answered, We are justified in assuming Theism true, because we are justified in assuming that known mind can *only* have been caused by an unknown mind, and hence that Mind must somewhere be self-existing, then this is to lead us to the second objection to the above syllogism.

§ 12. And this second objection is of a most serious nature. "Mind can only be caused by Mind," and, therefore, Mind must either be uncaused, or caused by a creating Mind. What is our warrant for making this assertion? Where is the proof that nothing can have caused a mind except another mind? Answer to this question there is none. For aught that we can ever know to the contrary, anything within the whole range of the Possible may be competent to produce a self-conscious intelligence—and to assume that Mind is so far an entity *sui generis*, that it must either be self-existing, or derived from another mind which is self-existing, is merely to beg the whole question as to the being of a God. In other words, if we can prove that the order of existence to which Mind belongs, is so essentially different from that order, or those orders, to which all else belongs, as to render it *abstractedly impossible* that the latter can produce the former—if we can prove this, we have likewise proved the existence of a Deity. But this is just the point in dispute, and to set out with a bare affirmation of it is merely to beg the question and to abandon the discussion. Doubtless, by the mere act of consulting their own consciousness, the fact now in dispute appears to some persons self-evident. But in matters of such high abstraction as this, even the evidence of self-evidence must not be relied upon too implicitly. To the country boor it appears self-evident that wood is annihilated by combustion; and even to the mind of the greatest philosophers of antiquity it seemed impossible to doubt that the sun moved over a stationary earth. Much more, therefore, may our broad distinction between "cogitative and incogitative being"[1] not be a distinction which is "legitimated by the conditions of external reality."

Doubtless many will fall back upon the position already indicated, "It is as repugnant to the idea of senseless matter, that it should put into itself sense, perception, and knowledge, as it is repugnant to the idea of a triangle, that it should put into itself greater angles than two right ones." But, granting this, and also that conscious matter is the sole alternative, and what follows? Not surely that matter cannot perceive, and feel, and know, merely because it is repugnant to our idea of it that it should. Granting that there is no other alternative in the whole possibility of things, than that matter must be conscious, or that self-conscious Mind must somewhere be self-existing; and granting that it is quite "impossible for us to conceive" of consciousness as an attribute of matter; still surely it would be a prodigious leap to conclude that for this reason matter cannot possess this attribute. Indeed, Locke himself elsewhere strangely enough insists that thought may be a property of matter, if only the Deity chose to unite that attribute with that substance. Why it should be deemed abstractedly impossible for matter to think if there is no God, and yet abstractedly possible that it should think if there is a God, I confess myself quite unable to determine; but I conceive that it is very important clearly to point out this peculiarity in Locke's views, for he is a favourite authority with theists, and this peculiarity amounts to nothing less than a suicide of his entire argument. The mere circumstance that he assumed the Deity capable of endowing matter with the faculty of thinking, could not have enabled him to *conceive* of matter as thinking, any

[1] Locke, *loc. cit.*

more than he could *conceive* of this in the absence of his assumption. Yet in the one case he recognises the possibility of matter thinking, and in the other case denies such possibility, *and this on the sole ground of its being inconceivable!* However, I am not here concerned with Locke's eccentricities:[1] I am merely engaged with the general principle, that a subjective inability to establish certain relations in thought is no sufficient warrant for concluding that corresponding objective relations may not obtain.

§ 13. Hence, an objector to the above syllogism need not be a materialist; it is not even necessary that he should hold any theory of things at all. Nevertheless, for the sake of definition, I shall assume that he is a materialist. As a materialist, then, he would appear to be as much entitled to his hypothesis as a theist is to his—in respect, I mean, of this particular argument. For although I think, as before shown, that in strict reasoning a theist might have taken exception to the last-quoted passage from Mill in its connection with the law of causation, that passage, if considered in the present connection, is certainly unanswerable. What is the state of the present argument as between a materialist and a theist? The mystery of existence and the inconceivability of matter thinking are their common data. Upon these data the materialist, justly arguing that he has no right to make his own conceptive faculty the unconditional test of objective possibility, is content to merge the mystery of his own mind's existence into that of Existence in general; while the theist, compelled to accept without explanation the mystery of Existence in general, nevertheless has recourse to inventing a wholly gratuitous hypothesis to explain one mode of existence in particular. If it is said that the latter hypothesis has the merit of causing the mystery of material existence and the mystery of mental existence to be united in a thinkable manner—

[1] See Appendix A.

viz., in a self-existing Mind,—I reply, It is not so; for in whatever degree it is unthinkable that Matter should be the cause of Mind, in that precise degree must it be unthinkable that Mind was ever the cause of Matter, the correlatives being in each case the same, and experience affording no evidence of causality in either.

§ 14. The two hypotheses, therefore, are of exactly equivalent value, save that while the one has a certain basis of fact to rest upon,[1] the other is wholly arbitrary.

[1] Viz., the constant association within experience of mind with certain highly peculiar material forms; the constant proportion which is found to subsist between the quantity of cerebral matter and the degree of intellectual capacity—a proportion which may be clearly traced throughout the ascending series of vertebrated animals, and which is very generally manifested in individuals of the human species; the effects of cerebral anæmia, anæsthetics, stimulants, narcotic poisons, and lesions of cerebral substance. There can, in short, be no question that the whole series of observable facts bearing upon the subject are precisely such as they ought to be upon supposition of the materialistic theory being true; while, contrariwise, there is a total absence of any known facts tending to negative that theory. At the same time it must be carefully noted, that the observed facts (and any additional number of the like kind) do not logically warrant us in concluding that mental states are necessarily *dependent* upon material changes. Nevertheless, it must also be noted, that, in the absence of positive proof of causation, it is certainly in accordance with scientific procedure, to yield our provisional assent to an hypothesis which undoubtedly connects a large order of constant *accompaniments*, rather than to an hypothesis which is confessedly framed to meet but a single one of the facts.

Professor Clifford, in a lecture on "Body and Mind" which he delivered at St. George's Hall, and afterwards published in the *Fortnightly Review*, argues against the existence of God on the ground that, as Mind is always associated with Matter within experience, there arises a presumption against Mind existing anywhere without being thus associated, so that unless we can trace in the disposition of the heavenly bodies some resemblance to the conformation of cerebral structure, we are to conclude that there is a considerable balance of probability in favour of Atheism. Now, as this argument—if we rid it of the grotesque allusion to the heavenly bodies—is one that is frequently met with, it seems desirable in this place briefly to analyse it. First of all, then, the validity of the argument depends upon the probability there is that the constant association of Mind with Matter within experience is due to a *causal* connection; for if the association in question is merely an *association* and nothing more, the origin of known mind is as far from being explained as it would be were Mind never known as associated with Matter. But, in the next place, supposing the constant association in question to be due to a causal connection, it by no means follows that because Mind is due to Matter within experience, therefore Mind cannot exist in any other mode beyond experience.

B

But it may still be retorted, 'Is not that which is *most* conceivable *most likely* to be true? and if it is more conceivable that my intelligence is caused by another Intelligence than that it is caused by Non-intelligence, may I not regard the more conceivable hypothesis as also the more probable one?' It is somewhat difficult to say how far this argument is, in this case, valid; only I think it is quite evident that its validity is open to grave dispute. For nothing can be more evident to a philosophical thinker than that the substance of Mind must—so far at least as we can at present see—*necessarily* be unknowable; so that if Matter (and Force) be this substance, we should antecedently expect to find that the actual causal connection should, in this particular case, be more inconceivable than some imaginary one: it would be more natural for the mind to infer that something conceivably more akin to itself should be its cause, than that this cause should be the entity which really gives rise to the unthinkable connection. But even waiving this reflection, and granting that the above argument is *valid*, it is still to an indefinite degree *valueless*, seeing that we are unable to tell *how much it is more likely* that the more conceivable should here be true than that the less conceivable should be so.

Doubtless, from analogy, there is a presumption against the hypothesis that the same entity should exist in more than one mode at the same time; but clearly in this case we are quite unable to estimate the value of this presumption. Consequently, even assuming a causal connection between Matter and Human Mind, if there is any, the slightest, indications supplied by any other facts of experience pointing to the existence of a Divine Mind, such indications should be allowed as much argumentative weight as they would have had in the absence of the presumption we are considering. Hence Professor Clifford's conclusion cannot be regarded as valid until all the other arguments in favour of Theism have been separately refuted. Doubtless Professor Clifford will be the first to recognise the cogency of this criticism —if indeed it has not already occurred to him; for as I know that he is much too clear a thinker not to perceive the validity of these considerations, I am willing to believe that the substance of them was omitted from his essay merely for the sake of brevity; but, for the sake of less thoughtful persons, I have deemed it desirable to state thus clearly that the problem of Theism cannot be solved on grounds of Materialism alone. [This note was written before I had the advantage of Professor Clifford's acquaintance, but I now leave it, as I leave all other parts of this essay—viz., as it was originally written.—1878.]

§ 15. Returning then to Locke's comparison between the certainty of this argument and that which proves the sum of the angles of a triangle to be equal to two right-angles, I should say that there is a *virtual*, though not a *formal*, fallacy in his presentation. For mathematical science being confessedly but of relative significance, any comparison between the degree of certainty attained by reasoning upon so transcendental a subject as the present, and that of mathematical demonstrations regarding relative truth, must be misleading. In the present instance, the whole strain of the argument comes upon the adequacy of the proposed test of truth, viz., our being able to conceive it if true. Now, will any one undertake to say that this test of truth is of equivalent value when it is applied to a triangle and when it is applied to the Deity. In the one case we are dealing with a geometrical figure of an exceedingly simple type, with which our experience is well acquainted, and presenting a very limited number of relations for us to contemplate. In the other case we are endeavouring to deal with the *summum genus* of all mystery, with reference to which experience is quite impossible, and which in its mention contains all the relations that are to us unknown and unknowable. Here, then, is the oversight. Because men find conceivability a valid test of truth in the affairs of everyday life—as it is easy to show *à priori* that it must be, if our experience has been formed under a given code of constant and general laws—therefore they conclude that it must be equally valid *wherever* it is applied; forgetting that its validity must perforce decrease in proportion to the distance at which the test is applied from the sphere of experience.[1]

---

[1] To avoid burdening the text, I have omitted another criticism which may be made on Locke's argument. "Triangle" is a word by which we designate a certain figure, one of the properties of which is that the sum of its angles is equal to two right angles. In other words, any figure which does not exhibit this property is not that figure which we designate a triangle. Hence, when Locke says he cannot conceive of a triangle which does not present this property, it may be answered that

§ 16. Upon the whole, then, I think it is transparently obvious that the mere fact of our being unable to conceive, say, how any disposition of matter and motion could possibly give rise to a self-conscious intelligence, in no wise warrants us in concluding that for this reason no such disposition is possible. The only question would appear to be, whether the test whch is here proposed as an unconditional criterion of truth should be allowed any the smallest degree of credit. Seeing, on the one hand, how very fallible the test in question is known to have proved itself in many cases of much less speculative difficulty—seeing, too, that even now "the philosophy of the condition proves that things there are which may, nay must, be true, of which nevertheless the mind is unable to construe to itself the possibility;"[1] and seeing, on the

his inability arises merely from the fact that any figure which fails to present this property is not a figure to which the term "triangle" can apply. Thus viewed, however, the illustration would obviously be absurd, for the same reason that the question of the clown is absurd, "Can you think of a horse that is just like a cow?" What Locke evidently means is, that we cannot conceive of any geometrical figure which presents all the other properties of a triangle without also presenting the property in question. Now, even admitting, with Locke, that it is as inconceivable that the entity known to us as Matter should possess the property of causing thought as it is that the figure which we term a triangle should possess the property of containing more than two right angles, still it remains, for the purposes of Locke's supposed theistic demonstration, to prove that it is as inconceivable for the entity which we call Mind *not* to be due to another Mind, as it is for a triangle *not* to contain other than two right angles. But, further, even if it were possible to prove this, the demonstration would make as much against Theism as in favour of it; for if, as the illustration of the triangle implies, we restrict the meaning of the word "Mind" to an entity one of whose essential qualities is that it should be caused by another Mind, the words "Supreme and Uncaused Mind" involve a contradiction in terms, just as much as would the words "A square triangle having four right angles." It would, therefore, seem that if we adhere to Locke's argument, and pursue it to its conclusion, the only logical outcome would be this:—Seeing that by the word "Mind," I expressly connote the quality of derivation from a prior Mind, as a quality belonging no less essentially to Mind than the quality of presenting two right angles belongs to a triangle; therefore, whatever other attributes I ascribe to the First Cause, I must clearly exclude the attribute Mind; and hence, whatever else such a Cause may be, it follows from my argument that it certainly is—Not Mind.

[1] Hamilton.

other hand, that the substance of Mind, whatever it is, must necessarily be unknowable;—seeing these things, if any question remains as to whether the test of inconceivability should in this case be regarded as having any degree of validity at all, there can, I think, be no reasonable doubt that such degree should be regarded as of the smallest.

§ 17. Let us then turn to the other considerations which have been supposed to justify the assertion that nothing can have caused our mind save another Mind. Neglecting the crushing fact that "it does not account for Mind to refer it to another Mind for its origin," let us see what positive reasons there are for concluding that no other influence than Intelligence can possibly have produced our intelligence.

§ 18. First we may notice the argument which is well and tersely presented by Locke, thus:—"Whatsoever is first of all things must necessarily contain in it, and actually have, at least, all the perfections that can ever after exist; nor can it ever give to another any perfection that it hath not actually in itself, or at least in a higher degree; it necessarily follows that the first eternal being cannot be Matter." Now, as this presentation is strictly formal, I shall first meet it with a formal reply, and this reply consists in a direct contradiction. It is simply untrue that "whatsoever is first of all things must necessarily contain in it, and actually have, at least, all the perfections that can after exist;" or that it can never "give to another any perfection that it hath not actually in itself." In a sense, no doubt, a cause contains all that is contained in its effects; the latter content being *potentially* present in the former. But to say that a cause already contains *actually* all that its effects may afterwards so contain, is a statement which logic and common sense alike condemn as absurd.

Nevertheless, although the argument now before us thus admits of a childishly easy refutation on strictly formal grounds, I suspect that in substance the argument in a general way is often relied upon as one of very considerable weight. Even though it is clearly illogical to say that causes cannot give to their effects any perfection which they themselves do not actually present, yet it seems in a general way incredible that gross matter could contain, even potentially, the faculty of thinking. Nevertheless, this is but to appeal to the argument from Inconceivability; to do which, even were it here legitimate, would, as we have seen, be unavailing. But to appeal to the argument from Inconceivability in this case would *not* be legitimate; for we are in possession of an abundant analogy to render the supposition in question, not only conceivable, but credible. In the words of Mr. Mill, "Apart from experience, and arguing on what is called reason, that is, on supposed self-evidence, the notion seems to be that no causes can give rise to products of a more precious or elevated kind than themselves. But this is at variance with the known analogies of nature. How vastly nobler and more precious, for instance, are the vegetables and animals than the soil and manure out of which, and by the properties of which, they are raised up! The tendency of all recent speculation is towards the opinion that the development of inferior orders of existence into superior, the substitution of greater elaboration, and higher organisation for lower, is the general rule of nature. Whether this is so or not, there are at least in nature a multitude of facts bearing that character, and this is sufficient for the argument."

§ 19. We now come to the last of the arguments which, so far as I know, have ever been adduced in support of the assertion that there can be no other cause of our intelligence than another and superior Intelligence. The argument is chiefly remarkable for the very great prominence which was given to it by Sir W. Hamilton.

This learned and able author says:—"The Deity is not an object of immediate contemplation; as existing and in himself, he is beyond our reach; we can know him only mediately through his works, and are only warranted in assuming his existence as a certain kind of cause necessary to account for a certain state of things, of whose reality our faculties are supposed to inform us. The affirmation of a God being thus a regressive inference from the existence of a special class of effects to the existence of a special character of cause, it is evident that the whole argument hinges on the fact,—Does a state of things really exist such as is only possible through the agency of a Divine Cause? For if it can be shown that such a state of things does not really exist, then our inference to the kind of cause requisite to account for it is necessarily null.

"This being understood, I now proceed to show you that the class of phænomena which requires that kind of cause we denominate a Deity is exclusively given in the phænomena of mind,—that the phænomena of matter taken by themselves, (you will observe the qualification taken by themselves) so far from warranting any inference to the existence of a God, would, on the contrary, ground even an argument to his negation.

"If, in man, intelligence be a free power,—in so far as its liberty extends, intelligence must be independent of necessity and matter; and a power independent of matter necessarily implies the existence of an immaterial subject,—that is, a spirit. If, then, the original independence of intelligence on matter in the human constitution, in other words, if the spirituality of mind in man be supposed a datum of observation, in this datum is also given both the condition and the proof of a God. For we have only to infer, what analogy entitles us to do, that intelligence holds the same relative supremacy in the universe which it holds in us, and the first positive condition of a Deity is established in the establishment of the absolute priority of a free creative intelligence." [1]

§ 20. Thus, according to Sir W. Hamilton, the whole

[1] Lectures on Metaphysics, vol. i. pp. 25-31.

question as to the being of a God depends upon that as to whether our "intelligence be a free power,"—or, as he elsewhere states it himself, "Theology is wholly dependent upon Psychology, for with the proof of the moral nature of man stands or falls the proof of the existence of a Deity." It will be observed that I am not at present engaged with the legitimacy of this author's decision upon the comparative merits of the different arguments in favour of Theism: I am merely showing the high opinion he entertained of the particular argument before us. He positively affirms that, unless the freedom of the human will be a matter of experience, Atheism is the sole alternative. Doubtless most well-informed readers will feel that the solitary basis thus provided for Theism is a very insecure one, while many such readers will at once conclude that if this is the only basis which reason can provide for Theism to stand upon, Theism is without any rational basis to stand upon at all. I have no hesitation in saying that the last-mentioned opinion is the one to which I myself subscribe, for I am quite unable to understand how any one at the present day, and with the most moderate powers of abstract thinking, can possibly bring himself to embrace the theory of Free-will. I may add that I cannot but believe that those who do embrace this theory with an honest conviction, must have failed to understand the issue to which modern thought has reduced the question. Here, however, is not the place to discuss this question. It will be sufficient for my purpose to show that even Sir W. Hamilton himself considered it a very difficult one; and although he thought upon the whole that the will must be free, he nevertheless allowed—nay, insisted—that he was unable to conceive how it could be so. Such inability in itself does not of course show the Free-will theory to be untrue; and I merely point out the circumstance that Hamilton allowed the supposed fact unthinkable, in order to show how very precarious, even in his eyes, the argument which we are considering must have appeared. Let us then, for this purpose, contemplate his attitude with regard to it a little more closely. He says, "It would have been better to show articulately that Liberty and Necessity are both incomprehensible, as beyond the limits of legitimate thought; but that though the Free-agency of Man cannot be speculatively proved, so neither can it be speculatively disproved; while we may claim for it as a fact of real actuality, though of inconceivable possibility, the testimony of consciousness, that we are morally free, as we are morally accountable for our actions. In this manner the whole question of free- and bond-will is in theory abolished, leaving, however, practically our Liberty, and all the moral instincts of Man entire."[1]

From this passage it is clear that Sir W. Hamilton regarded these two counter-theories as of precisely equivalent value in everything save "the testimony of consciousness;" or, as he elsewhere states it, "as equally unthinkable, the two counter, the two one-sided, schemes are thus theoretically balanced. But, practically, our consciousness of the moral law . . . gives a decisive preponderance to the doctrine of freedom over the doctrine of fate."

But the whole question concerning the freedom of the will has now come to be as to whether or not consciousness *does* give its verdict on the side of freedom. Supposing we grant that "we are warranted to rely on a deliverance of consciousness, when that deliverance is *that* a thing is, although we may be unable to think *how* it can be,"[2] in this case the question still remains, whether our opponents have rightly interpreted the deliverance of their consciousness. I, for one, am quite persuaded that I never perform any action without some appropriate motive, or set of motives, having induced me to perform it. However, I am not discussing this question, and I have merely made the above quotations

[1] Lectures on Metaphysics, vol. ii. p. 542.   [2] *Loc. cit.*, p. 543.

for the purpose of showing that Sir W. Hamilton appears to identify the *theory* of Free-will with the *fact* that we possess a moral sense. He argues throughout as though the theory he advocates were the only one that can explain a given " fact of real actuality." But no one with whom we have to deal questions the fact of our having a moral sense; and to identify this " deliverance of consciousness" with belief in the theory that volitions are uncaused, is, or would now be, merely to abandon the only questions in dispute.

It is very instructive, from this point of view, to observe the dilemma into which Hamilton found himself driven by this identification of genuine fact with spurious theory. He believed that the fact of man possessing an ethical faculty could only be explained by the theory that man's will was not determined by motives; for otherwise man could not be the author of his own actions. But when he considered the matter in its other aspect, he found that his theory of Free-will was as little compatible with moral responsibility as was the opposing theory of " Bond-will;" for not only did he candidly confess that he could not conceive of will as acting without motives, but he further allowed the unquestionable truth "that, though inconceivable, a motiveless volition would, if conceived, be conceived as morally worthless."[1] I say this is very instructive, because it shows that in Hamilton's view each theory was alike irreconcilable with " the deliverance of consciousness," and that he only chose the one in preference to the other, because, although not any more conceivable a solution, it seemed to him a more possible one.[2]

§ 21. Such, then, is the speculative basis on which, according to Sir W. Hamilton, our belief in a Deity can alone be grounded.

---

[1] Appendix to Discussions, pp. 614, 615.
[2] Mill, in the lengthy chapter which he devotes to the freedom of the will in his Examination, does not notice this point.

Those who at the present day are still confused enough in their notions regarding the Free-will question to suppose that any further rational question remains, may here be left to ruminate over this *bolus*, and to draw from it such nourishment as they can in support of their belief in a God; but to those who can see as plainly as daylight that the doctrine of Determinism not only harmonises with all the facts of observation, but alone affords a possible condition for, and a satisfactory explanation of, the existence of our ethical faculty,—to such persons the question will naturally arise :—" Although Hamilton was wrong in identifying a known fact with a false theory, yet may he not have been right in the deductions which he drew from the fact ?" In other words, granting that his theory of Freewill was wrong, does not his argument from the existence of a moral sense in man to the existence of a moral Governor of the Universe remain as intact as ever ? Now, it is quite true that whatever degree of cogency the argument from the presence of the moral sense may at any time have had, this degree remains unaffected by the explosion of erroneous theories to account for such presence. We have, therefore, still to face the fact that the moral sense of man undoubtedly exists.

§ 22. The question we have to determine is, What evidence have we to show that the moral part of man was created in the image of God; and if there is any such evidence, what counter-existence is there to show that the moral existence of man may be due to natural causes? In deciding this question, just as in deciding any other question of a purely scientific character, we must be guided in our examination by the Law of Parcimony ; we must not assume the agency of supernatural causes if we can discover the agency of natural causes ; neither must we merge the supposed mystery directly into the highest mystery, until we are quite sure that it does not admit of being proximately explained by the action of proximate influences.

Now, whether or not Mr. Darwin's theory as to the

origin and development of the moral sense be considered satisfactory, there can, I think, be very little doubt in any impartial mind which duly considers the subject, that in *some way or other* the moral sense has been evolved. The body of scientific evidence which has now been collected in favour of the general theory of evolution is simply overwhelming; and in the presence of so large an analogy, it would require a vast amount of contradictory evidence to remove the presumption that human conscience, like everything else, has been evolved. Now, for my own part, I am quite unable to distinguish any such evidence, while, on the other hand, in support of the *à priori* presumption that conscience has been evolved, I cannot conceal from myself that there is a large amount of *à posteriori* confirmation. I am quite unable to distinguish anything in my sense of right and wrong which I cannot easily conceive to have been brought about during the evolution of my intelligence from lower forms of psychical life. On the contrary, everything that I can find in my sense of right and wrong is precisely what I should expect to find on the supposition of this sense having been moulded by the progressive requirements of social development. Read in the light of evolution, Conscience, in its every detail, is deductively explained.

And, as though there were not sufficient evidence of this kind to justify the conclusion drawn from the theory of evolution, the doctrine of utilitarianism—separately conceived and separately worked out on altogether independent grounds—the doctrine of utilitarianism comes in with irresistible force to confirm that *à priori* conclusion by the widest and most unexceptionable of inductions.[1]

---

[1] If more evidence can be wanted, it is supplied in some suggestive facts of Psychology. For example, "From our earliest childhood, the idea of doing wrong (that is, of doing what is forbidden, or what is injurious to others) and the idea of punishment are presented to the mind together, and the intense character of the impressions causes the association between them to attain the highest degree of closeness and intimacy. Is

In the supernatural interpretation of the facts, the whole stress of the argument comes upon the character of conscience as a *spontaneously admonishing influence which acts independently of our own volition.* For it is from this character alone that the inference can arise that conscience is the delegate of the will of another. Thus, to render the whole argument in the singularly beautiful words of Dr. Newman:—" If, as is the case, we feel responsibility, are ashamed, are frightened at transgressing the voice of conscience, this implies that there is One to whom we are responsible, before whom we are ashamed, whose claims upon us we fear. If, on doing wrong, we feel the same tearful, broken-hearted sorrow which overwhelms us on hurting a mother; if, on doing right, we enjoy the same seeming serenity of mind, the same soothing, satisfactory delight, which follows on one receiving praise from a father,—we certainly have within us the image of some person to whom our love and veneration look, in whose smile we find our happiness, for whom we yearn, towards whom we direct our pleadings, in whose anger we waste away. These feelings in us are such as require for their exciting cause an intelligent being; we are not affectionate towards a stone, nor do we feel shame before a horse or a dog; we have no remorse or compunction in breaking mere human law. Yet so it is; conscience emits all these painful emotions, confusion, foreboding, self-condemnation; and, on the other hand, it sheds upon us a deep peace, a sense of security, a resignation, and a hope which there is no sensible, no earthly object to elicit. 'The

---

it strange, or unlike the usual processes of the human mind, that in these circumstances we should retain the feeling and forget the reason on which it is grounded? But why do I speak of forgetting? In most cases the reason has never, in our early education, been presented to the mind. The only ideas presented have been those of wrong and punishment, and an inseparable association has been created between these directly, without the help of any intervening idea. This is quite enough to make the spontaneous feelings of mankind regard punishment and a wrong-doer as naturally fitted to each other—as a conjunction appropriate in itself, independently of any consequences," &c.—Mill, Examination of Hamilton, p. 599.

wicked flees when no one pursueth;' then why does he flee? whence his terror? Who is it that he sees in solitude, in darkness, in the hidden chambers of his heart? If the cause of these emotions does not belong to this visible world, the Object to which his perception is directed must be supernatural and divine; and thus the phenomena of conscience as a dictate avail to impress the imagination with the picture of a Supreme Governor, a Judge, holy, just, powerful, all-seeing, retributive."[1]

Now I have quoted this passage because it seems to me to convey in a concise form the whole of the argument from Conscience. But how tremendous are the inferences which are drawn from the facts! As the first step in our criticism, it is necessary to point out that two very different orders of feelings are here treated by Dr. Newman. There is first the pure or uncompounded ethical feelings, which spring directly from the moral sense alone, and which all men experience in varying degrees. And next there are what we may term the *ethico-theological* feelings, which can only spring from a blending of the moral sense with a belief in a personal God, or other supernatural agents. The former class of feelings, or the uncompounded ethical class, have exclusive reference to the moral obligations that subsist between ourselves and other human beings, or sentient organisms. The latter class of feelings, or the ethico-theological class, have reference to the moral obligations that are believed to subsist between ourselves and the Deity, or other supernatural beings. Now, in order not to lose sight of this all-important distinction, I shall criticise Dr. Newman's rendering of the ordinary argument from Conscience in each of these two points of views separately. To begin, then, with the uncompounded ethical feelings.

Such emotions as attend the operation of conscience in those who follow its light alone, without any theories as to its supernatural origin, are all of the character of *reason-*

---

[1] Grammar of Assent, pp. 106, 107.

able or *explicable* emotions. Granting that fellow-feeling has been for the benefit of the race, and therefore that it has been developed by natural causes, certainly there is nothing *mysterious* in the emotions that attend the violating or the following of the dictates of conscience. For conscience is, by this naturalistic supposition, nothing more than an organised body of certain psychological elements, which, by long inheritance, have come to inform us, by way of intuitive feeling, how we should act for the interests of society; so that, if this hypothesis is correct, there cannot be anything more mysterious or supernatural in the working of conscience than there is in the working of any of our other faculties. That the disagreeable feeling of *self-reproach*, as distinguished from *religious* feeling, should follow upon a violation of such an organised body of psychological elements, cannot be thought surprising, if it is remembered that one of these elements is natural fellow-feeling, and the others the elements which lead us to know directly that we have violated the interests of other persons. And as regards the mere fact that the working of conscience is independent of the will, surely this is not more than we find, in varying degrees, to be true of all our emotions; and conscience, according to the evolution theory, has its root in the emotions. Hence, it is no more an argument to say that the irrepressible character of conscience refers us to a God of morality, than it would be to say that the sometimes resistless force of the ludicrous refers us to a god of laughter. Love, again, is an emotion which cannot be subdued by volition, and in its tendency to persist bears just such a striking resemblance to the feelings of morality as we should expect to find on the supposition of the former having played an important part in the genesis of the latter. The *dictating* character of conscience, therefore, is clearly in itself of no avail as pointing to a superhuman Dictator. Thus, for example, to take Dr. Newman's own illustration, why should we feel such tearful, broken-hearted sorrow on intentionally or carelessly hurting a mother? We see no shadow of a reason for resorting to any supernatural hypothesis to explain the fact—love between mother and offspring being an essential condition to the existence of higher animals. Yet this is a simple case of truly conscientious feeling, where the thought of any *personal* cause of conscience *need* not be entertained, and is certainly not necessary to explain the effects. And similarly with *all* cases of conscientious feeling, *except in cases where it refers directly to its supposed author*. But these latter cases, or the ethico-theological class of feelings, are in no way surprising. If the moral sense has had a natural genesis in the actual relations between man and man, as soon as an ideal "image" of "a holy, just, powerful, all-seeing, retributive" God is firmly believed to have an objective existence, as a matter of course moral feelings must become transferred to the relations which are believed to obtain between ourselves and this most holy God. Indeed, it is these very feelings which, in the absence of any proof to the contrary, must be concluded, in accordance with the law of parcimony, to have *generated* this idea of God as "holy, just," and good. And the mere fact that, when the complex system of religious belief has once been built up, conscience is strongly wrought upon by that belief and its accompanying emotions, is surely a fact the very reverse of mysterious. Suppose, for the sake of argument, that the moral sense has been evolved from the social feelings, and should we not certainly expect that, when the belief in a moral and all-seeing God is superadded, conscience should be distracted at the thought of offending him, and experience a "soothing, satisfactory delight" in the belief that we are pleasing him? And as to the argument, "Why does the wicked flee when none pursueth? whence his terror?" the question admits of only too easy an answer. Indeed, the form into which the question is thrown would almost seem —were it not written by Dr. Newman—to imply a sarcastic reference to the power of superstition. "Who is it that," not only Dr. Newman, but the haunted savage, the mediæval sorcerer, or the frightened child, "sees in solitude, in darkness, in the hidden chambers of his heart?" Who but the "image" of his own thought? "If the cause of these emotions does not belong to this visible world, the Object to which his perception is directed must be supernatural and divine." Assuredly; but what an inference from what an assumption! Whether or not the moral sense has been developed by natural causes, "these emotions" of terror at the thought of offending beings "supernatural and divine" are not of such unique occurrence "in the visible world" as to give Dr. Newman the monopoly of his particular "Object." With a deeper meaning, therefore, than he intends may we repeat, "The phenomena of conscience as a dictate *avail* to impress the *imagination* with the *picture* of a Supreme Governor." But criticism here is positively painful. Let it be enough to say that those of us who do not already believe in any such particular "Object"—be it ghost, shape, demon, or deity—are strangers, utter and complete, to any such supernatural pursuers. The fact, therefore, of these various religious emotions being associated with conscience in the minds of theists, can in itself be no proof of Theism, seeing that it is the theory of Theism which itself *engenders* these emotions; those who do not believe in this theory experiencing none of these feelings of personal dread, responsibility to an unknown God, and the feelings of doing injury to, or of receiving praise from, a parent. To such of us the violation of conscience is its own punishment, as the pursuit of virtue is its own reward. For we know that not more certainly than fire will burn, any violation of the deeply-rooted feelings of our humanity will leave a gaping wound which even time may not always heal. And when it is shown us that our natural dread of fire is due to a supernatural cause, we may be prepared to entertain the argument that our natural dread of sin, as distinguished from our dread of God, is likewise due to such a cause. But until this can be done we must, as reasonable men, *whose minds have been trained in the school of nature,* forbear to allow that the one fact is of any greater cogency than the other, so far as the question of a supernatural cause of either is concerned. For, as we have already seen, the law of parcimony forbids us to ascribe "the phenomena of conscience as a dictate" to a supernatural cause, until the science of psychology shall have proved that they cannot have been due to natural causes. But, as we have also seen, the science of psychology is now beginning, as quick and thoroughly as can be expected, to prove the very converse; so that the probability is now overwhelming that our moral sense, like all our other faculties, has been evolved. Therefore, while the burden of proof really lies on the side of Theism—or with those who account for the natural phenomena of conscience by the hypothesis of a supernatural origin—this burden is now being rapidly discharged by the opposite side. That is to say, while the proofs which are now beginning to substantiate the naturalistic hypothesis are all in full accord with the ordinary lines of scientific explanations, the vague and feeble reflections of those who still maintain that Conscience is evidence of Deity, are all such as run counter to the very truisms of scientific method.

In the face of all the facts, therefore, I find it impossible to recognise as valid any inference which is drawn from the existence of our moral sense to the existence of a God; although, of course, all inferences drawn from the existence of our moral sense to the *character* of a God already believed to exist remain unaffected by the foregoing considerations.[1]

[1] Throughout these considerations I have confined myself to the *positive* side of the subject. My argument being of the nature of a criticism on the erroneous inferences which are drawn from the *good* qualities of our moral nature, I thought it desirable, for the sake of clearness, not to bur-

den that argument by the additional one as to the source of the *evil* qualities of that nature. This additional argument, however, will be found briefly stated at the close of my supplementary essay on Professor Flint's "Theism." On reading that additional argument, I think that any candid and unbiassed mind must conclude that, alike in what it is *not* as well as in what it *is*, our moral nature points to a natural genesis, as distinguished from a supernatural cause.

CHAPTER III.

THE ARGUMENT FROM DESIGN.

§ 23. THE argument from Design, as presented by Mill, is merely a resuscitation of it as presented by Paley. True it is that the logical penetration of the former enabled him to perceive that the latter had "put the case much too strongly;" although, even here, he has failed to see wherein Paley's error consisted. He says:—"If I found a watch on an apparently desolate island, I should indeed infer that it had been left there by a human being; but the inference would not be from the marks of design, but because I already know by direct experience that watches are made by men." Now I submit that this misses the whole point of Paley's meaning; for it is evident that there would be no argument at all unless this author be understood to say what he clearly enough expresses, viz., that the evidence of design supposed to be afforded by the watch is supposed to be afforded by examination of its mechanism only, and not by any previous knowledge as to how that particular mechanism called a watch is made. Paley, I take it, only chose a watch for his example because he knew that no reader would dispute the fact that watches are constructed by design: except for the purpose of pointing out that mechanism is in some cases admitted to be due to intelligence, for all the other purposes of his argument he might as well have chosen for his illustration any case of mechanism occurring in nature. What the real fallacy in Paley's argument is, is another question, and this I shall now endeavour to answer; for, as Mill's argument is clearly the same in kind as that of Paley and his numberless followers, in examining the one I am also examining the other.

§ 24. In nature, then, we see innumerable examples of apparent design: are these of equal value in testifying to the presence of a designing intelligence as are similar examples of human contrivance, and if not, why not? The answer to the first of these questions is patent. If such examples were of the same value in the one case as they are in the other, the existence of a Deity would be, as Paley appears to have thought it was, demonstrated by the fact. A brief and yet satisfactory answer to the second question is not so easy, and we may best approach it by assuming the existence of a Deity. If, then, there is a God, it by no means follows that every apparent contrivance in nature is an actual contrivance, in the same sense as is any human contrivance. The eye of a vertebrated animal, for instance, exhibits as much apparent design as does a watch; but no one—at the present day, at least—will undertake to affirm that the evidence of divine thought furnished by one example is as conclusive as is the evidence of human thought furnished by the other—and this even assuming a Deity to exist. Why is this? The reason, I think, is, that we know by our personal experience what are our own relations to the material world, and to the laws which preside over the action of physical forces; while we can have no corresponding knowledge of the relations subsisting between the Deity and these same objects of our own experience. Hence, to suppose that the Deity constructed the eye by any such process of thought as we know that men construct watches, is to make an assumption not only incapable of proof, but destitute of any assignable degree of likelihood. Take an example. The relation in which a bee stands to the external world is to a large extent a matter of observation, and, therefore, no one imagines that the formation of its scientifically-constructed cells is due to any profound study on the bee's part. Whatever the origin of the cell-making instinct may have been, its nature is certainly not the same as it would have been in man, supposing him to have had occasion to construct honeycombs. It may be said that the requisite calculations have been made for the bees by the Deity; but, even if this assumption were true, it would be nothing to the point, which is merely that even within the limits of the animal kingdom the relations of intelligence to the external world are so diverse, that the same results may be accomplished by totally different intellectual processes. And as this example is parallel to the case on which we are engaged in everything save the *observability* of the relations involved, it supplies us with the exact measure of the probability we are trying to estimate. Hence it is evident that so long as we remain ignorant of the element essential to the argument from design in its Paleyerian form—viz., knowledge or presumption of the relations subsisting between an hypothetical Deity and his creation—so long must that argument remain, not only unassignably weak, but incapable of being strengthened by any number of examples similar in kind.

§ 25. To put the case in another way. The root fallacy in Paley's argument consisted in reasoning from a particular to an universal. Because he knew that design was the cause of adaptation in some cases, and because the phenomena of life exhibited more instances of adaptation than any other class of phenomena in nature, he pointed to these phenomena as affording an exceptional kind of proof of the presence in nature of intelligent agency. Yet, if it is admitted—and of this, even in Paley's days, there was a strong analogical presumption—that the phenomena of life are throughout their history as much subject to law as are any other phenomena whatsoever,—that the method of the divine government, supposing such to exist, is the same here as elsewhere; then nothing can be clearer than that any amount of observable adaptation of means to ends within this class of phenomena cannot afford any different kind of evidence of *design* than is afforded by any other class of phenomena whatsoever. Either we know the relations of the Deity to his creation, or we do not. If we do, then we must know whether or not *every* physical change which occurs in accordance with law—*i.e.*, every change occurring within experience, and so, until contrary evidence is produced, presumably every change occurring beyond experience—was separately planned by the Deity. If we do not, then we have no more reason to suppose that any one set of physical changes rather than another has been separately planned by him, unless we could point (as Paley virtually pointed) to one particular set of changes and assert, These are not subject to the same method of divine government which we observe elsewhere, or, in other words, to law. If it is retorted that *in some way or other* all these wonderful adaptations must ultimately have been due to intelligence, this is merely to shift the argument to a ground which we shall presently have to consider: all we are now engaged upon is to show that we have no right to found arguments on the assumed *mode, manner*, or *process* by which the supposed intelligence is thought to have operated. We can here see, then, more clearly where Paley stumbled. He virtually assumed that the relations subsisting between the Deity and the universe were such, that the exceptional adaptations met with in the organised part of the latter cannot have been due to the same intellectual *processes* as was the rest of the universe—or that, if they were, still they yielded better evidence of having been due to these processes than does the rest of the universe. And it is easy to perceive that his error arose from his pre-formed belief in special creation. So long as a man regards every living organism which he sees as the lineal descendant of a precisely similar organism originally struck out by the immediate fiat of Deity, so long is he justified in holding his axiom, "Contrivance must have had a contriver." For "adaptation" then becomes to our minds the synonym of "contrivance"—it being utterly inconceivable that the numberless adaptations found in any living organism could have resulted in any other way than by intelligent contrivance, at the time when this organism was in the first instance *suddenly* introduced into its complex conditions of life. Still, as an argument, this is of course merely reasoning in a circle: we adopt a hypothesis which presupposes the existence of a Deity as the first step in the proof of his existence. I do not say that Paley committed this error expressly, but merely that if it had not been for his pre-formed conviction as to the truth of the special-creation theory, he would probably not have written his "Natural Theology."

§ 26. Thus let us take a case of his own choosing, and the one which is adduced by him as typical of "the application of the argument." "I know of no better method of introducing so large a subject than that of comparing a single thing with a single thing; an eye, for example, with a telescope. As far as the examination of the instrument goes, there is precisely the same proof that the eye was made for vision as there is that the telescope was made for assisting it. They are both made upon the same principles, both being adjusted to the laws by which the transmission and refraction of rays of light are regulated. I speak not of the origin of the laws themselves; but these laws being fixed, the construction in both cases is adapted to them. For instance: these laws require, in order to produce the same effect, that the rays of light, in passing through water into the eye, should be refracted by a more convex surface than when it passes out of air into the eye. Accordingly we find that the eye of a fish, in that part of it called the crystalline lens, is much rounder than the eye of terrestrial animals. What plainer manifestation of design can there be than this difference?" But what, let us ask, is the proximate cause of this difference? 'The immediate volition of the Deity, manifested in special creation,' virtually answers Paley; while we of to-day are able to reply, 'The agency of natural laws, to wit, inheritance, variation, survival of the fittest, and probably of other laws as yet not discovered.' Now, of course, according to the former of these two premises, there can be no more legitimate conclusion than that the difference in question is due to intelligent and special design; but, according to the other premise, it is equally clear that no conclusion can be more unwarranted; for, under the latter view, the greater rotundity of the crystalline lens in a fish's eye no more exhibits the presence of any special design than does the adaptation of a river to the bed which it has itself been the means of excavating. When, therefore, Paley goes on to ask:—"How is it possible, under circumstances of such close affinity, and under the operation of equal evidence, to exclude contrivance from the case of the eye, yet to acknowledge the proof of contrivance having been employed, as the plainest and clearest of all propositions, in the case of the telescope?" the answer is sufficiently obvious, namely, that the "evidence" in the two cases is *not* "equal;"—any more than is the existence, say, of the Nile of equal value in point of evidence that it was designed for traffic, as is the existence of the Suez Canal that it was so designed. And the mere fact that the problem of achromatism was solved by "the mind of a sagacious optician inquiring how this matter was managed in the eye," no more proves that "this could not be in the eye without purpose, which suggested to the optician the only effectual means of attaining that purpose," than would the fact, say, of the winnowing of corn having suggested the fanning-machine prove that air currents were designed for the purpose of eliminating chaff from grain. In short, the real substance of the argument from Design must eventually merge into that which Paley, in the above-quoted passage, expressly passes over—viz., "the origin of the laws themselves;" for so long as there is any reason to suppose that any apparent "adaptation" to a certain set of "fixed laws" is itself due to the influence of other "fixed laws," so long have we as little right to say that the latter set of fixed laws exhibit any better indications of intelligent adaptation to the former set, than the former do to that of the latter—the eye to light, than light to the eye. Hence I conceive that Mill is entirely wrong when he says of Paley's argument, "It surpasses analogy exactly as induction surpasses it," because "the instances chosen are particular instances of a circumstance which experience shows to have a real connection with an intelligent origin—the fact of conspiring to an end." Experience shows us this, but it shows us more besides; it shows us that there is no *necessary* or *uniform* connection between an "intelligent origin" and the fact of apparent "means conspiring to an [apparent] end." If the reader will take the trouble to compare this quotation just made from Mill, and the long train of reasoning that follows, with an admirable illustration in Mr. Wallace's "Natural Selection," he will be well rewarded by finding all the steps in Mr. Mill's reasoning so closely paralleled by the caricature, that but for the respective dates of publication, one might have thought the latter had an express reference to the former.[1] True, Mr. Mill closes his argument with a brief allusion to the "principle of the survival of the fittest," observing that "creative forethought is not absolutely the only link by which the origin of the wonderful mechanism of the eye may be connected with the fact of sight." I am surprised, however, that a man of Mr. Mill's penetration did not see that whatever view we may take as to "the adequacy of this principle (*i.e.*, Natural Selection) to account for such truly admirable combinations as some of those in nature," the argument from *Design* is not materially affected. So

---

[1] The illustration to which I refer is that of the watershed of a country being precisely adapted to draining purposes. The rivers just fit their own particular beds: the latter occupy the lowest grounds, and get broader and deeper as they advance; pebbles, gravel, and sand all occupy the best teleological situations, &c., &c.

far as this argument is concerned, the issue is not Design *versus* Natural Selection, but it is Design *versus* Natural Law. By all means, "leaving this remarkable speculation (*i.e.*, Mr. Darwin's) to whatever fate the progress of discovery may have in store for it," and it by no means follows that "in the present state of knowledge the adaptations in nature afford a large balance of probability in favour of creation by intelligence." For whatever we may think of this special theory as to the *mode*, there can be no longer any reasonable doubt, "in the present state of our knowledge," as to the truth of the general theory of *Evolution;* and the latter, if accepted, is as destructive to the argument from *Design* as would the former be if proved. In a word, it is the *fact* and not the *method* of Evolution which is subversive of Teleology in its Paleyerian form.

§ 27. We have come then to this:—Apparent intellectual adaptations are perfectly valid indications of design, so long as their authorship is known to be confined to human intelligence; for then we know from experience what are our relations to these laws, and so in any given case can argue *à posteriori* that such an adaptation to such a set of laws by such an intelligence can only have been due to such a process. But when we overstep the limits of experience, we are not entitled to argue anything *à priori* of any other intelligence in this respect, even supposing any such intelligence to exist. The analogy by which the unknown relations are inferred from the known is "infinitely precarious;" seeing that two of the analogous terms—to wit, the divine intelligence and the human—may differ to an immeasurable extent in their properties—nay, are supposed thus to differ, the one being supposed omniscient, omnipotent, &c., and the other not. And, as a final step, we may now see that the argument from Design, in its last resort, resolves itself into a *petitio principii*. For, ultimately, the only point which the analogical argument in question is adduced to prove is, that the relations subsisting between an Unknown Cause and certain physical forces are so far identical with the relations known to subsist between human intelligence and these same forces, that similar intellectual processes are required in the two cases to account for the production of similar effects—and hence that the Unknown Cause is intelligent. But it is evident that the analogy itself can have no existence, except upon the presupposition that these two sets of relations *are* thus identical. The point which the analogy is adduced to prove is therefore postulated by the fact of its being adduced at all, and the whole argument resolves itself into a case of *petitio principii*.

CHAPTER IV.

THE ARGUMENT FROM GENERAL LAWS.

§ 28. TURNING now to an important error of Mr. Mill's in respect of omission, I firmly believe that all competent writers who have ever undertaken to support the argument from Design, have been moved to do so by their instinctive appreciation of the much more important argument, which Mill does not mention at all and which we now proceed to consider—the argument from General Laws. That is to say, I cannot think that any one competent writer ever seriously believed, had he taken time to analyse his beliefs, that the cogency of his argument lay in assuming any knowledge concerning the *process* of divine thought; he must have really believed that it lay entirely in his observation of the *product* of divine thought—or rather, let us say, of divine intelligence. Now this is the whole difference between the argument from Design and the argument from General Laws. The argument from Design says, There must be a God, because such and such an organic structure must have been due to such and such an intellectual *process*. The argument from General Laws says, There must be a God, because such and such an organic structure must *in some way or other have been ultimately due to* intelligence. Nor does this argument end here. Not only must such and such an organic structure have been ultimately due to intelligence, but every such structure—nay, every phenomenon in the universe—must have been the same; for all phenomena are alike subject to the same method of sequence. The argument is thus a cumulative one; for as there is no single known exception to this universal mode of existence, the united effect of so vast a body of evidence is all but irresistible, and its tendency is clearly to point us to some *one* explanatory cause. The scope of this argument is therefore co-extensive with the universe; it draws alike upon all phenomena with which experience is acquainted. For instance, it contains all the phenomena covered by the Design argument, just as a genus contains any one of its species; it being manifest, from what was said in the last section, that if the general doctrine of Evolution is accepted, the argument from Design must of necessity merge into that from General Laws. And this wide basis, we may be sure, must be the most legitimate one whereon to rest an argument in favour of Theism. If there is any such thing as such an argument at all, the most unassailable field for its display must be the universe as a whole, seeing that if we separate any one section of the universe from the rest, and suppose that we here discover a different kind of testimony to intelligence from that which we can discover elsewhere, we may from analogy be abundantly sure that on the confines of our division there must be second causes and general laws at work (whether discoverable or not), which are the immediate agents in the production of the observed results. Of course I do not deny that some classes of phenomena afford us more and better proofs of intellectual agency than do others, in the sense of the laws in operation being more numerous, subtle, and complex; but it will be seen that this is a different interpretation of the evidence from that against which I am contending. Thus, if there are tokens of divine intention (as distinguished from design) to be met with in the eye,—if it is inconceivable that so " nice and intricate a structure" should exist without intelligence as its *ultimate* cause; then the discovery of natural selection, or of any other law, as the *manner* in which this intelligence wrought in no wise attenuates the proof as to the fact of an intelligent cause. On the contrary, it tends rather to confirm it; for, besides the evidence before existing, there is added that which arises from the conformity of the method to that which is observable in the rest of the universe.

Thus, notwithstanding what Hamilton, Chalmers, and others have said, I cannot but feel that the ubiquitous action of general laws is, of all facts supplied by experience, the most cogent in its bearing upon teleology. If perpetual and uninterrupted uniformity of method does not indicate the existence of a presiding intelligence, it becomes a question whether any other kind of method —short of the intelligently miraculous—could possibly do so; seeing that the further the divine *modus operandi* (supposing such to exist) were removed from absolute uniformity, the greater would be the room for our interpreting it as mere fortuity. But forasmuch as the progress of science has shown that within experience the method of the Supreme Causality is absolutely uniform, the hypothesis of fortuity is rendered irrational; and let us think of this Supreme Causality as we may, the fact remains that from it there emanates a directive influence of uninterrupted consistency, on a scale of stupendous magnitude and exact precision, worthy of our highest possible conceptions of Deity.

§ 29. Had it been my lot to have lived in the last generation, I doubt not that I should have regarded the foregoing considerations as final: I should have concluded that there was an overwhelming balance of rational probability in favour of Theism; and I think I should also have insisted that this balance of rational probability would require to continue as it was till the end of time. I should have maintained, in some such words as the following, in which the Rev. Baden Powell conveys this argument:—" The very essence of the whole argument is the invariable preservation of the principle of *order:* not necessarily such as we can directly recognise, but the universal conviction of the unfailing subordination of everything to *some* grand principles of *law*, however imperfectly apprehended in our partial conceptions, and the successive subordination of such laws to others of still higher generality, to an extent transcending our conceptions, and constituting the true chain of universal causation which culminates in the sublime conception of the COSMOS.

"It is in immediate connection with this enlarged view of universal immutable natural order that I have regarded the narrow notions of those who obscure the sublime prospect by imagining so unworthy an idea as that of occasional interruptions in the physical economy of the world.

"The only instance considered was that of the alleged sudden supernatural origination of new species of organised beings in remote geological epochs. It is in relation to the broad principle of law, if once rightly apprehended, that such inferences are seen to be wholly unwarranted by science, and such fancies utterly derogatory and inadmissible in philosophy; while, even in those instances properly understood, the real scientific conclusions of the invariable and indissoluble chain of causation stand vindicated in the sublime contemplations with which they are thus associated.

"To a correct apprehension of the whole argument, the one essential requisite is to have obtained a complete and satisfactory grasp of this *one grand principle of law pervading nature, or rather constituting the very idea of nature;*—which forms the vital essence of the whole of inductive science, and the sole assurance of those higher inferences from the inductive study of natural causes which are the vindications of a supreme intelligence and a moral cause.

"*The whole of the ensuing discussion must stand or fall with the admission of this grand principle.* Those who are not prepared to embrace it in its full extent may probably not accept the conclusions; but they must be sent back to the school of inductive science, where alone it must be independently imbibed and thoroughly assimilated with the mind of the student in the first instance.

"On the slightest consideration of the nature, the foundations, and general results of inductive science, . . . we recognise the powers of intellect fitly employed in the study of nature, . . . pre-eminently leading us to perceive *in nature,* and in the invariable and universal constancy of its laws, the indications of universal, unchangeable, and recondite arrangement, dependence, and connection in reason. . . .

"We thus see the importance of taking a more enlarged view of the great argument of natural theology; and the necessity for so doing becomes the more apparent when we reflect on the injury to which these sublime inferences are exposed from the narrow and unworthy form in which the reasoning has been too often conducted. . . .

"The satisfactory view of the whole case can only be found in those more enlarged conceptions which are furnished by the grand contemplation of cosmical order and unity, and which do not refer to inferences from the *past,* but to proofs of the *ever-present* mind and reason in nature.

"If we read a book which it requires much thought and exercise of reason to understand, but which we find discloses more and more truth and reason as we proceed in the study, and contains clearly more than we can at present comprehend, then undeniably we properly say that thought and reason *exist in that book* irrespectively of our minds, and equally so of any question as to its author or origin. Such a book confessedly exists, and is ever open to us in the natural world. Or, to put the case under a slightly different form :—When the astronomer, the physicist, the geologist, or the naturalist notes down a series of observed facts or measured dates, he is not an *author* expressing his own ideas,—he is a mere *amanuensis* taking down the dictations of nature : his observation book is the record of the thoughts of *another mind :* he has but set down literally what he himself does not understand, or only very imperfectly. On further examination, and after deep and anxious study, he perhaps begins to decipher the meaning, by perceiving some law which gives a signification to the facts; and the further he pursues the investigation up to any more comprehensive theory, the more fully he perceives that there is a higher reason, of which his own is but the humbler interpreter, and into whose depths he may penetrate continually further, to discover yet more profound and invariable order and system, always indicating still deeper and more hidden abysses yet unfathomed, but throughout which he is assured the same recondite and immutable arrangement ever prevails.

"That which requires thought and reason to understand must be itself thought and reason. That which mind alone can investigate or express must be itself mind. And if the highest conception attained is but partial, then the mind and reason studied is greater than the mind and reason of the student. If the more it be studied the more vast and complex is the necessary connection in reason disclosed, then the more evident is the vast extent and compass of the intelligence thus partially manifested, and its reality, as *existing in the immutably connected order of objects examined*, independently of the mind of the investigator.

"But considerations of this kind, just and transcendently important as they are in themselves, give us no aid in any inquiry into the *origin* of the order of things thus investigated, or the *nature* or other attributes of the mind evinced in them.

"The real argument for universal *intelligence*, manifested in the universality of order and law in the material world, is very different from any attempt to give a form to our conceptions, even by the language of analogy, as to the *nature* or *mode of existence* or operation of that intelligence [*i.e.*, as I have stated the case, the argument can only rest on a study of the *products*, as distinguished from the *pro-*

cesses of such intelligence] : and still more different from any extension of our inference from what *is* to what *may have been*, from *present* order to a supposed *origination*, first adjustment, or planning of that order.

"By keeping these distinctions steadily in view, we appreciate properly both the limits and the extent and compass of what we may appropriately call COSMO-THEOLOGY."[1]

I have quoted these passages at length, because they convey in a more forcible, guarded, and accurate manner than any others with which I am acquainted, the strictly rational standing of this great subject prior to the date at which the above-quoted passage was written. Therefore, as I have said, if it had been my lot to have lived in the last generation, I should certainly have rested in these "sublime conceptions" as in an argument supreme and irrefutable. I should have felt that the progress of physical knowledge could never exert any other influence on Theism than that of ever tending more and more to confirm that magnificent belief, by continuously expanding our human thoughts into progressively advancing conceptions, ever grander and yet more grand, of that tremendous Origin of Things—the Mind of God. Such would have been my hope—such would have been my prayer. But now, how changed! Never in the history of man has so terrific a calamity befallen the race as that which all who look may now behold advancing as a deluge, black with destruction, resistless in might, uprooting our most cherished hopes, engulfing our most precious creed, and burying our highest life in mindless desolation. Science, whom erstwhile we thought a very Angel of God, pointing to that great barrier of Law, and proclaiming to the restless sea of changing doubt, "Hitherto shalt thou come, but no further, and here shall thy proud waves be stayed,"—even Science has now herself thrown down this trusted barrier; the

---

[1] "Order of Nature," by the Rev. Baden Powell, M.A., F.R.S., &c., 1859, pp. 228-241.

flood-gates of infidelity are open, and Atheism overwhelming is upon us.

§ 30. All and every law follows as a necessary consequence from the persistence of force and the primary qualities of matter.[1] That this must be so is evident if we consider that, were it not so, force could not be permanent nor matter constant. For instance, if action and reaction were not invariably equal and opposite, force would not be invariably persistent, seeing that in no case can the formula fail, unless some one or other of the forces concerned, or parts of them, disappear. And as with a simple law of this kind, so with every other natural law and inter-operation of laws, howsoever complex such inter-operation may be; for it is manifest that if in any case similar antecedents did not determine similar consequents, on one or other of these occasions some quantum of force, or of matter, or of both, must have disappeared—or, which is the same thing, the law of causation cannot have been constant. Every natural law, therefore, may be defined as the formula of a sequence, which must either ensue upon certain forces of a given intensity impinging upon certain given quantities, kinds, and forms of matter, or

[1] I think it desirable to state that I perceived this great truth before I was aware that it had been perceived also by Mr. Spencer. His statement of it now occurs in the short chapter of *First Principles* entitled "Relations between Forces." So far as I am able to ascertain, no one has hitherto considered this important doctrine in its immediate relation to the question of Theism.

In using the term "persistence of force," I am aware that I am using a term which is not unopen to criticism. But as Mr. Spencer's writings have brought this term into such general use among speculative thinkers, it seemed to me undesirable to modify it. Questions of mere terminology are without any importance in a discussion of this kind, provided that the terms are universally understood to mean what they are intended to mean; and I think that the signification which Mr. Spencer attaches to his term, "persistence of force," is sufficiently precise. Therefore, adopting his usage, whenever throughout the following pages I speak of force as persisting, what I intend to be understood is, that there is a something—call it force, or energy, or x—which, so far as experience or imagination can extend, is, in its relation to us, ubiquitous and illimitable; or, in other words, that it universally presents the property of permanence. (See, for a more detailed explanation, supplementary essay "On the Final Mystery of Things.")

else, by not ensuing, prove that the force or the matter concerned were not of a permanent nature.

§ 31. The argument, then, which was elaborated in § 29, and which has so long and so generally received the popular sanction in the common-sense epitome, that in the last record there must be mind in external nature, since "that which it requires thought and reason to understand must itself be thought and reason,"—this argument, I say, must now for ever be abandoned by reasonable men. No doubt it would be easy to point to several speculative thinkers who have previously combated this argument,[1] and from this fact some readers will perhaps be inclined to judge, from a false analogy, that as the argument in question has withstood previous assaults, it need not necessarily succumb to the present one. Be it observed, however, that the present assault differs from all previous assaults, just as demonstration differs from speculation. What has hitherto been but mere guess and unwarrantable assertion has now become a matter of the greatest certainty. That the argument from General Laws is a futile argument, is no longer a matter of unverifiable opinion: it is as sure as is the most fundamental axiom of science. That the argument will long remain in illogical minds, I doubt not; but that it is from henceforth quite inadmissible in accurate thinking, there can be no question. For the sake, however, of impressing this fact still more strongly upon such readers as have been accustomed to rely upon this argument, and so find it difficult thus

---

[1] Hamilton may here be especially noticed, because he went so far as to maintain that the phenomena of the external world, taken by themselves, would ground a valid argument to the negation of God. Although I cannot but think that this position was a conspicuously irrational one for any competent thinker to occupy before the scientific doctrine of the correlation of the forces had been enunciated, nevertheless I cannot lose the opportunity of alluding to this remarkable feature in Sir William Hamilton's philosophy, showing as it does that same prophetic forestalling of the results which have since followed from the discovery of the conservation of energy, as was shown by his no less remarkable theory of causation. (See supplementary essay "On the Final Mystery of Things.")

abruptly to reverse the whole current of their thoughts,—for the sake of such, I shall here add a few remarks with the view of facilitating the conception of an universal Order existing independently of Mind.

§ 32. Interpreting the mazy nexus of phenomena only by the facts which science has revealed, and what conclusion are we driven to accept? Clearly, looking to what has been said in the last two sections, that from the time when the process of evolution first began,—from the time before the condensation of the nebula had showed any signs of commencing,—every subsequent change or event of evolution was *necessarily bound* to ensue; else force and matter have not been persistent. How then, it will be asked, did the vast nexus of natural laws which is now observable ever begin or continue to be? In this way. When the first womb of things was pregnant with all the future, there would probably have been existent at any rate not more than one of the formulæ which we now call natural laws. This one law, of course, would have been the law of gravitation. Here we may take our stand. It does not signify whether there ever was a time when gravitation was not,—*i.e.*, if ever there was a time when matter, *as we now know it*, was not in existence;—for if there ever was such a time, there is no reason to doubt, but every reason to conclude, that the evolution of matter, as we now know it, was accomplished in accordance with law. Similarly, we are not concerned with the question as to how the law of gravitation came to be associated with matter; for it is overwhelmingly probable, from the extent of the analogy, that if our knowledge concerning molecular physics were sufficiently great, the existence of the law in question would be found to follow as a necessary deduction from the primary qualities of matter and force, just as we can now see that, when present, its peculiar quantitative action necessarily follows from the primary qualities of space.

Starting, then, with these data,—matter, force, and the

law of gravitation,—what must happen? We have the strongest scientific reason to believe that the matter of the solar system primordially existed in a highly diffused or nebulous form. By mutual gravitation, therefore, all the substance of the nebula must have begun to concentrate upon itself, or to condense. Now, from this point onwards, I wish it to be clearly understood that the mere consideration of the supposed facts not admitting of scientific proof, or of scientific explanation if true, in no wise affects the certainty of the doctrine which these facts are here adduced to establish. Fully granting that the alleged facts are not beyond dispute, and that, even if true, innumerable other unknown and unknowable facts must have been associated with them—fully admitting, in short, that our ideas concerning the genesis of the solar system are of the crudest and least trustworthy character; still, if it be admitted, what at the present day only ignorance or prejudice can deny, viz., that, as a whole, evolution has been the method of the universe; then it follows that the doctrine here contended for is as certainly true as it would be were we fully acquainted with every cause and every change which has acted and ensued throughout the whole process of the genesis of things.

Now, bearing this caveat in mind, we have next to observe that when once the nebula began to condense, new relations among its constituent parts would, *for this reason*, begin to be established. "Given a rare and widely diffused mass of nebulous matter, . . . what are the successive changes that will take place? Mutual gravitation will approximate its atoms, but their approximation will be opposed by atomic repulsion, the overcoming of which implies the evolution of heat." That is to say, the condensation of the nebula as a whole of necessity implies at least the origination of these new material and dynamical relations among its constituent parts. "As fast as this heat partially escapes by radiation, further approximation will take place, attended by further evolution of heat, and so on continuously: the processes not occurring separately, as here described, but simultaneously, uninterruptedly, and with increasing activity." Hence the newly established relations continuously acquire new increments of intensity. But now observe a more important point. The previous essential conditions remaining unaltered—viz., the persistence of matter and force, as well as, or rather let us say and consequently, the law of gravitation—these conditions, I say, remaining constant, and the newly established relations would necessarily *of themselves* give origin to *new* laws. For whenever two given quantities of force and matter met in one of the novel relations, they would of necessity give rise to novel effects; and whenever, on any future occasion, similar quantities of force and matter again so met, precisely similar effects would of necessity require to occur: but the occurrence of similar effects under similar conditions is all that we mean by a natural law.

Continuing, then, our quotation from Mr. Herbert Spencer's terse and lucid exposition of the nebular theory, we find this doctrine virtually embodied in the next sentences:—" Eventually this slow movement of the atoms towards their common centre of gravity will bring about phenomena of another order.

"Arguing from the known laws of atomic combination, it will happen that, when the nebulous mass has reached a particular stage of condensation—when its internally situated atoms have approached to within certain distances, have generated a certain amount of heat, and are subject to a certain mutual pressure (the heat and pressure increasing as the aggregation progresses), some of them will suddenly enter into chemical union. Whether the binary atoms so produced be of kinds such as we know, which is possible, or whether they be of kinds simpler than any we know, which is more probable, matters not to the argument. It suffices that molecular combinations of some species will finally take place." We have, then, here a new and important change of relations. Matter, primordially uniform, has itself become heterogeneous; and in as many places as it has thus changed its state, it must, in virtue of the fact, give rise to other hitherto novel relations, and so, in many cases, to new laws.[1]

It would be tedious and unnecessary to trace this genesis of natural law any further: indeed, it would be quite impossible so to trace it for any considerable distance without feeling that the ever-multiplying mazes of relations renders all speculation as to the actual processes quite useless. This fact, however, as before insisted, in no wise affects the only doctrine which I here enunciate—viz., that the self-generation of natural law is a necessary corollary from the persistence of matter and force. And that this must be so is now, I hope, sufficiently evident. Just as in the first dawn of things, when the proto-binary compounds of matter gave rise to new relations together with their appropriate laws, so throughout the whole process of evolution, as often as matter acquired a hitherto novel state, or in one of its old states entered into hitherto novel relations, so often would non-existent or even impossible laws become at once possible and necessary. And in this way I cannot see that there is any reason to stop until we arrive at all the marvellous complexity of things as they are. For aught that speculative reason can ever from henceforth show to the contrary, the evolution of all the diverse phenomena of inorganic nature, of life, and of mind, appears to be as necessary and as self-determined as is the being of that mysterious Something which is Everything,—the Entity we must all believe in, which without condition and beyond relation holds its existence in itself.

§ 33. Does it still seem incredible that, notwithstanding it requires mental processes to interpret external nature, external nature may nevertheless be destitute of mind? Then let us look at the subject on its obverse aspect.

---

[1] [Mr. N. Lockyer's work is now supplying important evidence on these points.—1878.]

According to the theory of evolution—which, be it always remembered, is no mere gratuitous supposition, but a genuine scientific theory—human intelligence, like everything else, has been evolved. Now in what does the evolution of intelligence consist? Any one acquainted with the writings of our great philosopher can have no hesitation in answering: Clearly and only in the establishment of more and more numerous and complex internal or psychological relations. In other words, the law of intelligence being "that the strengths of the inner cohesions between psychical states must be proportionate to the persistences of the outer relations symbolised," it follows that the development of intelligence is "secured by the one simple principle that experience of the outer relations *produces* inner cohesions, and makes the inner cohesions strong in proportion as the outer relations are persistent." Now the question before us at present is merely this:—Must we not infer that these outer relations are regulated by mind, seeing that order is undoubtedly apparent among them, and that it requires mental processes on our part to interpret this order? The only legitimate answer to this question is, that these outer relations *may* be regulated by mind, but that, in view of the evolution theory, we are certainly not entitled to infer that they *are* so regulated, *merely* because it requires mental processes on our part to interpret their orderly character. For if it is true that the human mind was itself evolved by these outer relations—ever continuously moulded into conformity with them as the prime condition of its existence—then its process of interpreting them is but reflecting (as it were) in consciousness these outer relations by which the inner ones were originally produced. Granting that, as a matter of fact, an objective macrocosm exists, and if we can prove or render probable that this objective macrocosm is *of itself* sufficient to evolve a subjective microcosm, I do not see any the faintest reason for the latter to conclude that a self-conscious intelligence is inherent in the former, merely because it is able to trace in the macrocosm some of those orderly objective relations by which its own corresponding subjective relations were originally produced. If it is said that it is impossible to conceive how, apart from mind, the orderly objective relations themselves can ever have originated, I reply that this is merely to shift the ground of discussion to that which occupied us in the last section : all we are now engaged upon is,—Granting that the existence of such orderly relations is actual, whether with or without mind to account for them ; and granting also that these relations are *of themselves* sufficient to produce corresponding subjective relations; then the mere fact of our conscious intelligence being able to discover numerous and complex outer relations answering to those which they themselves have caused in our intelligence, does not warrant the latter in concluding that the causal connection between intelligence and non-intelligence has ever been reversed—that these outer relations in turn are caused by a similar conscious intelligence. How such a thing as a conscious intelligence is possible is another and wholly unanswerable question (though not more so than that as to the existence of force and matter, and would not be rendered less so by merging the fact in a hypothetical Deity); but granting, as we must, that such an entity does exist, and supposing it to have been evolved by natural causes, then it would appear incontestably to follow, that whether or not objective existence is presided over by objective mind, our subjective mind would *alike* and *equally* require to read in the facts of the external world an indication, whether true or false, of some such presiding agency. The subjective mind being, by the supposition, but the obverse aspect of the sum total of such among objective relations as have had a share in its production, when, as in observation and reflection, this obverse aspect is again inverted upon its die, it naturally fits more or less exactly into all the prints.

§ 34. This last illustration, however, serves to introduce us to another point. The supposed evidence from which the existence of mind in nature is inferred does not always depend upon such minute correspondences between subjective method and objective method as the illustration suggests. Every natural theologian has experienced more or less difficulty in explaining the fact, that while there is a tolerably general similarity between the contrivances due to human thought and the apparent contrivances in nature which he regards as due to divine thought, the similarity is nevertheless *only* general. For instance, if a man has occasion to devise any artificial appliance, he does so with the least possible cost of labour to himself, and with the least possible expenditure of material. Yet it is obvious that in nature as a whole no such economic considerations obtain. Doubtless by superficial minds this assertion will be met at first with an indignant denial: they have been accustomed to accumulate instances of this very principle of economy in nature; perhaps written about it in books, and illustrated it in lectures,—totally ignoring the fact that the instances of economy in nature bear no proportion at all to the instances of prodigality. Conceive of the force which is being quite uselessly expended by all the wind-currents which are at this moment blowing over the face of Europe. Imagine the energy that must have been dissipated during the secular cooling of this single planet. Feebly try to think of what the sun is radiating into space. If it is retorted that we are incompetent to judge of the purposes of the Almighty, I reply that this is but to abandon the argument from economy whenever it is found untenable: we presume to be competent judges of almighty purposes so long as they appear to imitate our own; but so soon as there is any divergence observable, we change front. By thus selecting all the instances of economy in nature, and disregarding all the vastly greater instances of reckless waste, we are merely laying ourselves open to the charge of an unfair eclecticism. And this formal refutation of the argument from economy admits of being further justified in a strikingly substantial manner; for if all the examples of economy in nature that were ever observed, or admit being observed, were collected into one view, I undertake to affirm that, without exception, they would be found to marshal themselves in one great company—the subjects whose law is *survival of the fittest*. One question only will I here ask. Is it possible at the present day for any degree of prejudice, after due consideration, to withstand the fact that the solitary exceptions to the universal prodigality so painfully conspicuous in nature are to be found where there is also to be found a full and adequate physical explanation of their occurrence?

But, again, prodigality is only one of several particulars wherein the modes and the means of the supposed divine intelligence differ from those of its human counterpart. Comparative anatomists can point to organic structures which are far from being theoretically perfect: even the mind of man in these cases, notwithstanding its confessed deficiencies in respect both of cognitive and cogitative powers, is competent to suggest improvements to an intelligence supposed to be omniscient and all-wise! And what shall we say of the numerous cases in which the supposed purposes of this intelligence could have been attained by other and less roundabout means? In short, not needlessly to prolong discussion, it is admitted, even by natural theologians themselves, that the difficulties of reconciling, even approximately, the supposed processes of divine thought with the known processes of human thought are quite insuperable. The fact is expressed by such writers in various ways,—*e.g.*, that it would be presumptuous in man to expect complete conformity in all cases; that the counsels of God are past finding out; that his ways are not as our ways, and so on. Observing only, as before, that in thus ignoring adverse cases natural theologians are guilty of an unfair eclecticism, it is evident that all such expressions concede the fact, that even in those provinces of nature where the evidence of superhuman intelligence appears most plain, the resemblance of its apparent products to those of human intelligence consists in a general approximation of method rather than in any precise similarity of particulars: the likeness is generic rather than specific.

Now this is exactly what we should expect to be the case, if the similarity in question be due to the cause which the present section endeavours to set forth. If all natural laws are self-evolved, and if human intelligence is but a subjective photograph of certain among their interrelations, it seems but natural that when this photograph compares itself with the whole external world from parts of which it was taken, its subjective lights and shadows should be found to correspond with some of the objective lights and shadows much more perfectly than with others. Still there would doubtless be sufficient general conformity to lead the thinking photograph to conclude that the great world of objective reality, instead of being the *cause* of such conformity as exists, was itself the *effect* of some common cause,—that it too was of the nature of a picture. Dropping the figure, if it is true that human intelligence has been evolved by natural law, then in view of all that has been said it must now, I think, be tolerably apparent, *that as by the hypothesis human intelligence has always been required to think and to act in conformity with law, human intelligence must at last be in danger of confusing or identifying the fact of action in conformity with law with the existence and the action of a self-conscious intelligence. Reading then in external nature innumerable examples of action in conformity with law, human intelligence falls back upon the unwarrantable identification, and out of the bare fact that law exists in nature concludes that beyond nature there is an Intelligent Lawgiver.*

§ 35. From what has been said in the last five sections, it manifestly follows that all the varied phenomena of the universe not only may, but must, depend upon the persistence of force and the primary qualities of matter.[1] Be it remembered that the object of the last three sections was merely to *"facilitate conception"* of the fact that it does not at all follow, because the phenomena of external nature admit of being intelligently inquired into, therefore they are due to an intelligent cause. The last three sections are hence in a manner parenthetical, and it is of comparatively little importance whether or not they have been successful in their object; for, from what went before, it is abundantly manifest that, whether or not the subjective side of the question admits of satisfactory elucidation, there can be no doubt that the objective side of it is as certain as are the fundamental axioms of science. It does not admit of one moment's questioning that it is as certainly true that all the exquisite beauty and melodious harmony of nature follow as necessarily and as inevitably from the persistence of force and the primary qualities of matter, as it is certainly true that force is persistent, or that matter is extended and impenetrable. No doubt this generalisation is too vast to be adequately conceived, but there can be equally little doubt that it is necessarily true. If matter and force have been eternal, so far as human mind can soar it can discover no need of a superior mind to explain the varied phenomena of existence. Man has truly become in a new sense the measure of the universe, and in this the latest and most appalling of his soundings, indications are returned from the infinite voids of space and time by which he is surrounded, that his intelligence, with all its noble capacities for love and adoration, is yet alone—destitute of kith or kin in all this universe of being.

[1] It will of course be observed that if matter and force are identical, the unification is complete.

CHAPTER V.

THE LOGICAL STANDING OF THE QUESTION AS TO THE BEING OF A GOD.

§ 36. But the discussion must not end here. Inexorable logic has forced us to conclude that, viewing the question as to the existence of a God only by the light which modern science has shed upon it, there no longer appears to be any semblance of an argument in its favour. Let us then turn upon science herself, and question her right to be our sole guide in this matter. Undoubtedly we have no alternative but to conclude that the hypothesis of mind in nature is now logically proved to be as certainly superfluous as the very basis of all science is certainly true. There can no longer be any more doubt that the existence of a God is wholly unnecessary to explain any of the phenomena of the universe, than there is doubt that if I leave go of my pen it will fall upon the table. Nay, the doubt is even less than this, because while the knowledge that my pen will fall if I allow it to do so is founded chiefly upon empirical knowledge (I could not predict with *à priori* certainty that it would so fall, for the pen might be in an electrical state, or subject to some set of unknown natural laws antagonistic to gravity), the knowledge that a Deity is superfluous as an explanation of anything, being grounded on the doctrine of the persistence of force, is grounded on an *à priori* necessity of reason—*i.e.*, if this fact were not so, our science, our thought, our very existence itself, would be scientifically impossible.

But now, having thus stated the case as strongly as I am able, it remains to question how far the authority of science extends. Even our knowledge of the persistence of force and of the primary qualities of matter is but of relative significance. Deeper than the foundations of our experience, "deeper than demonstration—deeper even than definite cognition,—deep as the very nature of mind,"[1] are these the most ultimate of known truths; but where from this is our warrant for concluding with certainty that these known truths are everywhere and eternally true? It will be said that there is a strong analogical probability. Perhaps so, but of this next: I am not now speaking of probability; I am speaking of certainty; and unless we deny the doctrine of the relativity of knowledge, we cannot but conclude that there is no absolute certainty in this case. As I deem this consideration one of great importance, I shall proceed to develop it at some length. It will be observed, then, that the consideration really amounts to this:— Although it must on all hands be admitted that the fact of the theistic hypothesis not being required to explain any of the phenomena of nature is a fact which has been demonstrated *scientifically*, nevertheless it must likewise on all hands be admitted that this fact has not, and cannot be, demonstrated *logically*. Or thus, although it is unquestionably true that so far as science can penetrate she cannot discern any speculative necessity for a God, it may nevertheless be true that if science could penetrate further she might discern some such necessity. Now the present discussion would clearly be incomplete if it neglected to define as carefully this the logical standing of our subject, as it has hitherto endeavoured to define its scientific standing. As a final step in our analysis, therefore, we must altogether quit the region of experience, and, ignoring even the very foundations of science and so all the most certain of relative truths, pass into the transcendental

[1] **Herbert Spencer.**

region of purely formal considerations. In this region theist and atheist must alike consent to forego all their individual predilections, and, after regarding the subject as it were in the abstract and by the light of pure logic alone, finally come to an agreement as to the transcendental probability of the question before them. Disregarding the actual probability which they severally feel to exist in relation to their own individual intelligences, they must apply themselves to ascertain the probability which exists in relation to those fundamental laws of thought which preside over the intelligence of our race. In fine, it will now, I hope, be understood that, as we have hitherto been endeavouring to determine, by deductions drawn from the very foundations of all possible science, the *relative* probability as to the existence of a God, so we shall next apply ourselves to the task of ascertaining the *absolute* probability of such existence—or, more correctly, what is the strictly *formal* probability of such existence when its possibility is contemplated in an absolute sense.

§ 37. To begin then. In the last resort, the value of every probability is fixed by "ratiocination." In endeavouring, therefore, to fix the degree of strictly formal probability that is present in any given case, our method of procedure should be, first to ascertain the ultimate ratios on which the probability depends, and then to estimate the comparative value of these ratios. Now I think there can be no doubt that the value of any probability in this its last analysis is determined by the number, the importance, and the definiteness of the relations known, as compared with those of the relations unknown; and, consequently, that in all cases where the sum of the unknown relations is larger, or more important, or more indefinite than is the sum of the known relations, it is an essential principle that the value of the probability decreases in exact proportion to the decrease in the similarity between the two sets of relations, whether this decrease consists in the number, in the importance, or in the definiteness of the relations involved. This rule or canon is self-evident as soon as pointed out, and has been formulated by Professor Bain in his "Logic" when treating of Analogy, but not with sufficient precision; for, while recognising the elements of number and importance, he has overlooked that of definiteness. This element, however, is a very essential one—indeed the most essential of the three; for there are many analogical inferences in which either the character or the extent of the unknown relations is quite indefinite; and it is obvious that, whenever this is the case, the value of the analogy is proportionably diminished, and diminished in a much more material particular than . it is when the diminution of value arises from a mere excess of the unknown relations over the known ones in respect of their number or of their importance. For it is evident that, in the latter case, however little value the analogy may possess, the exact degree of such value admits of being *determined;* while it is no less evident that, in the former case, we are precluded from estimating the value of the analogy at all, and this just in proportion to the indefiniteness of the unknown relations.

§ 38. Now the particular instance with which we are concerned is somewhat peculiar. Notwithstanding we have the entire sphere of human experience from which to argue, we are still unable to gauge the strictly logical probability of any argument whatsoever; for the unknown relations in this case are so wholly indefinite, both as to their character and extent, that any attempt to institute a definite comparison between them and the known relations is felt at once to be absurd. The question discussed, being the most ultimate of all possible questions, must eventually contain in itself all that is to man unknown and unknowable; the whole orbit of human knowledge is here insufficient to obtain a parallax whereby to institute the required measurements.

§ 39. I think it is desirable to insist upon this truth at

somewhat greater length, and, for the sake of impressing it still more deeply, I shall present it in another form. No one can for a single moment deny that, beyond and around the sphere of the Knowable, there exists the unfathomable abyss of the Unknowable. I do not here use this latter word as embodying any theory: I merely wish it to state the undoubted fact, which all must admit, viz., that beneath all our possible explanations there lies a great Inexplicable. Now let us see what is the effect of making this necessary admission. In the first place, it clearly follows that, while our conceptions as to what the Unknowable contains may or may not represent the truth, it is certain that we can never discover whether or not they do. Further, it is impossible for us to determine even a definite *probability* as to the existence (much less the nature) of anything which we may suppose the Unknowable to contain. We may, of course, perceive that such and such a supposition is more *conceivable* than such and such; but, as already indicated, the fact does not show that the one is in itself more definitely *probable* than the other, unless it has been previously shown, either that the capacity of our conceptions is a *fully adequate measure* of the Possible, or that the proportion between such capacity and the extent of the Possible is a proportion that can be *determined*. In either of these cases, the Conceivable would be a fair measure of the Possible: in the former case, an exact equivalent (*e.g.*, in any instance of contradictory propositions, the most conceivable would *certainly* be true); in the latter case, a measure any degree less than an exact equivalent—the degree depending upon the *then* ascertainable disparity between the extent of the Possible and the extent of the Conceivable. Now the Unknowable (including of course the Inconceivable Existent) is a species of the Possible, and in its name carries the declaration that the disparity between its extent and the extent of the Conceivable (*i.e.*, the other species of the Possible) is a disparity that cannot be determined. We are hence driven to the conclusion that the most apparently probable of all propositions, if predicated of anything within the Unknowable, may not in reality be a whit more so than is the most apparently improbable proposition which it is possible to make; for if it is admitted (as of course it must be) that we are necessarily precluded from comparing the extent of the Conceivable with that of the Unknowable, then it necessarily follows that in no case whatever are we competent to judge how far an *apparent* probability relating to the latter province is an *actual* probability. In other words, did we know the proportion subsisting between the Conceivable and the Unknowable in respect of relative extent and character, and so of inherent probabilities, we should then be able to estimate the actual value of any apparent probability relating to the latter province; but, as it is, our ability to make this estimate varies inversely as our inability to estimate our ignorance in this particular. And as our ignorance in this particular is total—*i.e.*, since we cannot even approximately determine the proportion that subsists between the Conceivable and the Unknowable,—the result is that our ability to make the required estimate in any given case is absolutely *nil*.

§ 40. I have purposely rendered this presentation in terms of the highest abstraction, partly to avoid the possibility of any one, whatever his theory of things may be, finding anything at which to object, and partly in order that my meaning may be understood to include all things which are beyond the range of possible knowledge. Most of all, therefore, must this presentation (if it contains anything of truth) apply to the question regarding the existence of Deity; for the *Ens Realissimum* must of all things be furthest removed from the range of possible knowledge. Hence, if this presentation contains anything of truth— and of its rigidly accurate truth I think there can be no question—the assertion that the Self-existing Substance is a Personal and Intelligent Being, and the assertion that this Substance is an Impersonal and Non-Intelligent Being, are alike assertions wholly destitute of any assignable degree of logical probability. I say *assignable* degree of logical probability, because that *some* degree of such probability may exist I do not undertake to deny. All I assert is, that if we are here able to institute any such probability at all, we are unable logically to assign to it any determinate degree of value. Or, in other words, although we may establish some probability in a sense relative to ourselves, we are unable to know how far this probability is a probability in an absolute sense. Or again, the case is not as though we were altogether unacquainted with the Possible. Experience undoubtedly affords us some information regarding this, although, comparatively speaking, we are unable to know how much. Consequently, we must suppose that, in any given case, it is more likely that the Conceivable should be Possible than that the Inconceivable should be so, and that the Conceivably Probable should exist than that the Conceivably Improbable should do so: in neither case, however, can we know *what degree* of such likelihood is present.

§ 41. From the foregoing considerations, then, it would appear that the only attitude which in strict logic it is admissible to adopt towards the question concerning the being of a God is that of "suspended judgment." Formally speaking, it is alike illegitimate to affirm or to deny Intelligence as an attribute of the Ultimate. And here I would desire it to be observed, that this is the attitude which the majority of scientifically-trained philosophers actually have adopted with regard to this matter. I am not aware, however, that any one has yet endeavoured to formulate the justification of this attitude; and as I think there can be no doubt that the above presentation contains in a logical shape the whole of such justification, I cannot but think that some important ends will have been secured by it. For we are here in possession, not merely of a vague and general impression that the Ultimate is super-scientific, and so beyond the range of legitimate predication; but we are also in possession of a logical formula whereby at once to vindicate the rationality of our opinion, and to measure the precise degree of its technical value.

CHAPTER VI.

THE ARGUMENT FROM METAPHYSICAL TELEOLOGY.

§ 42. LET us now proceed to examine the effect of the formal considerations which have been adduced in the last chapter on the scientific considerations which were dealt with in the previous chapters. In these previous chapters the proposition was clearly established that, just as certainly as the fundamental data of science are true, so certainly is it true that the theory of Theism in any shape is, scientifically considered, superfluous; for these chapters have clearly shown that, if there is a God, his existence, considered as a cause of things, is as certainly unnecessary as it is certainly true that force is persistent and that matter is indestructible. But after this proposition had been carefully justified, it remained to show that the doctrine of the relativity of knowledge compelled us to carry our discussion into a region of yet higher abstraction. For although we observed that the essential qualities of matter and of force are the most ultimate data of human knowledge, and although, by showing how far the question of Theism depended on these data, we carried the discussion of that question to the utmost possible limits of scientific thought, it still devolved on us to contemplate the fact that even these the most ultimate data of science are only known to be of relative significance. And the bearing of this fact to the question of Theism was seen to be most important. For, without waiting to recapitulate the substance of a chapter so recently concluded, it will be remembered that its effect was to establish this position beyond all controversy—viz., that when ideas which have been formed by our experience within the region of phenomenal actuality are projected into the region of ontological possibility, they become utterly worthless; seeing that we can never have any means whereby to test the actual value of whatever transcendental probabilities they may appear to establish. Therefore it is that even the most ultimate of relative truths with which, as we have seen, the question of Theism is so vitally associated, is almost without meaning when contemplated in an absolute sense. What, then, is the effect of these metaphysical considerations on the position of Theism as we have seen it to be left by the highest generalisations of physical science? Let us contemplate this question with the care which it deserves.

In the first place, it is evident that the effect of these purely formal considerations is to render all reasonings on the subject of Theism equally illegitimate, unless it is constantly borne in mind that such reasonings can only be of relative signification. Thus, as a matter of pure logic, these considerations are destructive of all assignable validity of any such reasoning whatsoever. Still, even a strictly relative probability is, in some undefinable degree, of more value than no probability at all, as we have seen these same formal considerations to show (see § 40); and, moreover, even were this not so, the human mind will never rest until it attains to the furthest probability which to its powers is accessible. Therefore, if we do not forget the merely relative nature of the considerations which are about to be adduced, by adducing them we may at the same time satisfy our own minds and abstain from violating the conditions of sound logic.

The shape, then, to which the subject has now been reduced is simply this:—Seeing that the theory of Evolution in its largest sense has shown the theory of Theism to be superfluous in a scientific sense, does it not follow that the theory of Theism is thus shown to be superfluous in any sense? For it would seem from the discussion, so far as it has hitherto gone, that the only rational basis on which the theory of Theism can rest is a basis of teleology; and if, as has been clearly shown, the theory of evolution, by deducing the genesis of natural law from the primary data of science, irrevocably destroys this basis, does it not follow that the theory of evolution has likewise destroyed the theory which rested on that basis? Now I conclude, as stated at the close of Chapter IV., that the question here put must certainly be answered in the affirmative, so far as its scientific aspect is concerned. But when we consider the question in its purely logical aspect, as we have done in Chapter V., the case is otherwise. For although, so far as the utmost reach of scientific vision enables us to see, we can discern no evidence of Deity, it does not therefore follow that beyond the range of such vision Deity does not exist. Science indeed has proved that if there is a Divine Mind in nature, and if by the hypothesis such a Mind exerts any causative influence on the phenomena of nature, such influence is exerted beyond the sphere of experience. And this achievement of science, be it never forgotten, is an achievement of prodigious importance, effectually destroying, as it does, all vestiges of a scientific teleology. But be it now carefully observed, although all vestiges of a *scientific* teleology are thus completely and permanently ruined, the formal considerations adduced in the last chapter supply the conditions for constructing what may be termed a *metaphysical* teleology. I use these terms advisedly, because I think they will serve to bring out with great clearness the condition to which our analysis of the teleological argument has now been reduced.

§ 43. In the first place, let it be understood that I employ the terms "scientific" and "metaphysical" in the convenient sense in which they are employed by Mr. Lewes, viz., as respectively designating a theory that is verifiable and a theory that is not. Consequently, by the term "scientific teleology" I mean to denote a form of teleology which admits either of being proved or disproved, while by the term "metaphysical teleology" I mean to denote a form of teleology which does not admit either of being proved or of being disproved. Now, with these significations clearly understood, it will be seen that the forms of teleology which we have hitherto considered belong entirely to the scientific class. That the Paleyerian form of the argument did so is manifest, first because this argument itself treats the problem of Theism as a problem that is susceptible of scientific demonstration, and next because we have seen that the advance of science has proved this argument susceptible of scientific refutation. In other words, from the supposed axiom, "There cannot be apparent design without a designer," adaptations in nature become logically available as purely scientific evidence of an intelligent cause; and that Paley himself regarded them exclusively in this light is manifest, both from his own "statement of the argument," and from the character of the evidence by which he seeks to establish the argument when stated—witness the typical passage before quoted (§ 26). On the other hand, we have clearly seen that this Paleyerian system of natural theology has been effectually demolished by the scientific theory of natural selection—the fundamental axiom of the former having been shown by the latter to be scientifically untrue. Hence the term "scientific teleology" is without question applicable to the Paleyerian system.

Nor is the case essentially different with the more refined form of the teleological argument which we have had to consider—the argument, namely, from General Laws. For here, likewise, we have clearly seen that the inference from the ubiquitous operation of General Laws to the existence of an omniscient Law-maker is quite as illegitimate as is the inference from apparent Design to the existence of a supreme Designer. In other words, science, by establishing the doctrine of the persistence of force and the indestructibility of matter, has effectually disproved the hypothesis that the presence of Law in nature is of itself sufficient to prove the existence of an intelligent Law-giver.

Thus it is that scientific teleology in any form is now and for ever obsolete. But not so with what I have termed metaphysical teleology. For as we have seen that the doctrine of the relativity of knowledge precludes us from asserting, or even from inferring, that beyond the region of the Knowable Mind does not exist, it remains logically possible to institute a metaphysical hypothesis that beyond this region of the Knowable Mind does exist. There being a necessary absence of any positive information whereby to refute this metaphysical hypothesis, any one who chooses to adopt it is fully justified in doing so, provided only he remembers that the purely metaphysical quality whereby the hypothesis is ensured against disproof, likewise, and in the same degree, precludes it from the possibility of proof. He must remember that it is no longer open to him to point to any particular set of general laws and to assert, these proclaim Intelligence as their cause; for we have repeatedly seen that the known states of matter and force themselves afford sufficient explanation of the facts to which he points. And he must remember that the only reason why his hypothesis does not conflict with any of the truths known to science, is because he has been careful to rest that hypothesis upon a basis of purely formal considerations, which lie beyond even the most fundamental truths of which science is cognisant.

Thus, for example, he may present his metaphysical theory of Theism in some such terms as these:—'Fully conceding what reason shows must be conceded, and there still remains this possible supposition—viz., that there is a presiding Mind in nature, which exerts its causative influence beyond the sphere of experience, thus rendering it impossible for us to obtain scientific evidence of its action. For such a Mind, exerting such an influence beyond experience, may direct affairs within experience by methods conceivable or inconceivable to us—producing, possibly, innumerable and highly varied results, which in turn may produce their effects within experience, their introduction being then, of course, in the ordinary way of natural law. For instance, there can be no question that by the intelligent creation or dissipation of energy, all the phenomena of cosmic evolution might have been directed, and, for aught that science can show to the contrary, thus only rendered possible. Hence there is at least one nameable way in which, even in accordance with observed facts, a Supreme Mind could be competent to direct the phenomena of observable nature. But we are not necessarily restricted to the limits of the nameable in this matter, so that it is of no argumentative importance whether or not this suggested method is the method which the supposed Mind actually adopts, seeing that there may still be other possible methods, which, nevertheless, we are unable to suggest.'

Doubtless the hypothesis of Theism, as thus presented, will be deemed by many persons but of very slender probability. I am not, however, concerned with whatever character of probability it may be supposed to exhibit. I am merely engaged in carefully presenting the only hypothesis which can be presented, if the theory as to an Intelligent Author of nature is any longer to be maintained on grounds of a rational teleology. No doubt, scientifically considered, the hypothesis in question is purely gratuitous; for, so far as the light of science can penetrate, there is no need of any such hypothesis at all. Thus it may well seem, at first sight, that no hypothesis could well have less to recommend it; and, so far as the presentation has yet gone, it is therefore fully legitimate for an atheist to reply:—'All that this so-called metaphysical theory amounts to is a wholly gratuitous assumption. No doubt it is always difficult, and usually impossible, logically or unequivocally to prove a negative. If my adversary chose to imagine that nature is presided over by a demon with horns and hoofs, or by a dragon with claws and tail, I should be as unable to disprove this his supposed theory as I am now unable to disprove his actual theory. But in all cases reasonable men ought to be guided in their beliefs by such positive evidence as is available; and if, as in the present case, the alternative belief is wholly gratuitous—adopted not only without any evidence, but against all that great body of evidence which the sum-total of science supplies—surely we ought not to hesitate for one moment in the choice of our creed?'

Now all this is quite sound in principle, provided only that the metaphysical theory of Theism *is* wholly gratuitous, in the sense of being utterly destitute of evidential support. That it is destitute of all *scientific* support, we have already and repeatedly seen; but the question remains as to whether it is similarly destitute of *metaphysical* support.

§ 44. To this question, then, let us next address ourselves. From the theistic pleading which we have just heard, it is abundantly manifest that the formal conditions of a metaphysical teleology are present: the question now before us is as to whether or not any actual evidence exists in favour of such a theory. In order to discuss this question, let us begin by allowing the theist to continue his pleading. 'You have shown me,' he may say, 'that a scientific or demonstrable system of teleology is no longer possible, and, therefore, as I have already conceded, I must take my stand on a metaphysical or non-demonstrable system. But I reflect that the latter term is a loose one, seeing that it embraces all possible degrees of evidence short of actual proof. The question, therefore, I conceive to be, What amount of evidence is there in favour of this metaphysical system of teleology? And this question I answer by the following considerations:—

As general laws separately have all been shown to be the necessary outcome of the primary data of science, it certainly follows that general laws collectively must be the same—*i.e.*, that the whole system of general laws must be, so far as the lights of our science can penetrate, the necessary outcome of the persistence of force and the indestructibility of matter. But you have also clearly shown me that these lights are of the feeblest conceivable character when they are brought to illuminate the final mystery of things. I therefore feel at liberty to assert, that if there is any one principle to be observed in the collective operation of general laws which cannot conceivably be explained by any cause other than that of intelligent guidance, I am still free to fall back on such a principle and to maintain—Although the collective operation of general laws follows as a necessary consequence from the primary data of science, this one principle which pervades their united action, and which cannot be conceivably explained by any hypothesis other than that of intelligent guidance, is a principle which still remains to be accounted for; and as it cannot conceivably be accounted for on grounds of physical science, I may legitimately account for it on grounds of metaphysical teleology. Now I cannot open my eyes without perceiving such a principle everywhere characterising the collective operation of general laws. Universally I behold in nature, order, beauty, harmony,—that is, a perfect *correlation* among general laws. But this ubiquitous correlation among general laws, considered as the cause of cosmic harmony, itself requires some explanatory cause such as the persistence of force and the indestructibility of matter cannot conceivably be made to supply. For unless we postulate some one integrating cause, the greater the number of general laws in nature, the less likelihood is there of such laws being so correlated as to produce harmony by their combined action. And forasmuch as the only cause that I am able to imagine as competent to produce such effects is that of intelligent guidance, I accept the metaphysical hypothesis that beyond the sphere of the Knowable there exists an Unknown God.[1]

'If it is retorted that the above argument involves an absurd contradiction, in that while it sets out with an explicit avowal of the fact that the collective operation of general laws follows as a necessary consequence from the primary data of physical science, it nevertheless afterwards proceeds to explain an effect of such collective operation by a metaphysical hypothesis; I answer that it was expressly for the purpose of eliciting this retort that I threw my argument into the above form. For the position which I wish to establish is this, that fully accepting the logical cogency of the reasoning whereby the action of every law is deduced from the primary data of science, I wish to show that when this train of reasoning is followed to its ultimate term, it leads us into the presence of a fact for which it is inadequate to account. If, then, my contention be granted—viz., that to human faculties it is not conceivable how, in the absence of a directing intelligence, general laws could be so corre-

[1] It may here be observed that the above discussion would not be affected by the view of Professor Clifford and others, that natural law is to be regarded as having a subjective rather than an objective signification—that what we call a natural law is merely an arbitrary selection made by ourselves of certain among natural processes. The discussion would not be affected by this view, because the argument is really based upon the existence of a cosmos as distinguished from a chaos; and therefore it would be rather an intensification of the argument than otherwise to point out that, for the maintenance of a cosmos, natural laws, as conceived by us, would be inadequate. And this seems a fitting place to make the almost superfluous remark, that throughout this present essay I have used the words "Natural Law," "Supreme Law-giver," &c., in an apparently unguarded sense, merely in order to avoid needless obscurity. Fully sensible as I am of the misleading nature of the analogy which these words embody, I have yet adopted them for the sake of perspicuity — being careful, however, never to allow the false analogy which they express to enter into an argument on either side of the question. Thus, even where it is said that the existence of Natural Law points to the existence of a Supreme Law-maker, the argument might equally well be phrased: The existence of an orderly cosmos points to the existence of a disposing mind.

lated as to produce universal harmony—then I have brought the matter to this issue:—Notwithstanding the scientific train of argument being complete in itself, it still leaves us in the presence of a fact which it cannot conceivably explain; and it is this unexplained residuum—this total product of the operation of general laws—that I appeal to as the logical justification for a system of metaphysical teleology—a system which offers the only conceivable explanation of this stupendous fact.

'And here I may further observe, that the scientific train of reasoning is of the kind which embodies what Mr. Herbert Spencer calls "symbolic conceptions of the illegitimate order."[1] That is to say, we can see how such simple laws as that action and reaction are equal and opposite may have been self-evolved, and from this fact we go on generalising and generalising, until we land ourselves in wholly symbolic and—a paradox is here legitimate—inconceivable conceptions. Now the farther we travel into this region of unrealisable ideas, the less trustworthy is the report that we are able to bring back. The method is in a sense scientific; but when even scientific method is projected into a region of really super-scientific possibility, it ceases to have that character of undoubted certainty which it enjoys when dealing with verifiable subjects of inquiry. The demonstrations are formal, but they are not real.

'Therefore, looking to this necessarily suspicious character of the scientific train of reasoning, and then observing that, even if accepted, it leaves the fact of cosmic harmony unexplained, I maintain that whatever probability the phenomena of nature may in former times have been thought to establish in favour of the theory as to an intelligent Author of nature, that probability has been in no wise annihilated—nor apparently can it ever be annihilated—by the advance of science. And not only so, but I question whether this probability has been

[1] First Principles, pp. 27-29.

even seriously impaired by such advance, seeing that although this advance has revealed a speculative *raison d'être* of the mechanical precision of nature, it has at the same time shown the baffling complexity of nature; and therefore, in view of what has just been said, leaves the balance of probability concerning the existence of a God very much where it always was. For stay awhile to contemplate this astounding complexity of harmonious nature! Think of how much we already know of its innumerable laws and processes, and then think that this knowledge only serves to reveal, in a glimmering way, the huge immensity of the unknown. Try to picture the meshwork of contending rhythms which must have been before organic nature was built up, and then let us ask, Is it conceivable, is it credible, that all this can have been the work of blind fate? Must we not feel that had there not been intelligent agency at work somewhere, other and less terrifically intricate results would have ensued? And if we further try to symbolise in thought the unimaginable complexity of the material and dynamical changes in virtue of which that thought itself exists,—if we then extend our symbols to represent all the history of all the orderly changes which must have taken place to evolve human intelligence into what it is,—and if we still further extend our symbols to try if it be possible, even in the language of symbols, to express the number and the subtlety of those natural laws which now preside over the human will;—in the face of so vast an assumption as that all this has been self-evolved, I am content still to rest in the faith of my forefathers.'

§ 45. Now I think it must be admitted that we have here a valid argument. That is to say, the considerations which we have just adduced must, I think, in fairness be allowed to have established this position:—That the system of metaphysical teleology for which we have supposed a candid theist to plead, is something more than a purely gratuitous system—that it does not belong to the same category of baseless imaginings as that to which the atheist at first sight, and in view of the scientific deductions alone, might be inclined to assign it. For we have seen that our supposed theist, while fully admitting the formal cogency of the scientific train of reasoning, is nevertheless able to point to a fact which, in his opinion, lies without that train of reasoning. For he declares that it is beyond his powers of conception to regard the complex harmony of nature otherwise than as a product of some one integrating cause; and that the only cause of which he is able to conceive as adequate to produce such an effect is that of a conscious Intelligence. Pointing, therefore, to this complex harmony of nature as to a fact which cannot to his mind be conceivably explained by any deductions from physical science, he feels that he is justified in explaining this fact by the aid of a metaphysical hypothesis. And in so doing he is in my opinion perfectly justified, at any rate to this extent—that his antagonist cannot fairly dispose of this metaphysical hypothesis as a purely gratuitous hypothesis. How far it is a probable hypothesis is another question, and to this question we shall now address ourselves.

§ 46. If it is true that the deductions from physical science cannot be conceived to explain some among the observed facts of nature, and if it is true that these particular facts admit of being conceivably explained by the metaphysical hypothesis in question, then, beyond all controversy, this metaphysical hypothesis must be provisionally accepted. Let us then carefully examine the premises which are thus adduced to justify acceptance of this hypothesis as their conclusion.

In the first place, it is not—cannot—be denied, even by a theist, that the deductions from physical science *do* embrace the fact of cosmic harmony in their explanation, seeing that, as they explain the operation of general laws collectively, they must be regarded as also explaining every effect of such operation. And this, as we have seen, is a consideration to which our imaginary theist was not blind. How then did he meet it? He met it by the considerations—1st. That the scientific train of reasoning evolved this conclusion only by employing, in a wholly unrestricted manner, "symbolic conceptions of the illegitimate order;" and, 2d. That when the conclusion thus illegitimately evolved was directly confronted with the fact of cosmic harmony which it professes to explain, he found it to be beyond the powers of human thought to conceive of such an effect as due to such a cause. Now, as already observed, I consider these strictures on the scientific train of reasoning to be thoroughly valid. There can be no question that the highly symbolic character of the conceptions which that train of reasoning is compelled to adopt, is a source of serious weakness to the conclusions which it ultimately evolves; while there can, I think, be equally little doubt that there does not live a human being who would venture honestly to affirm, that he can really conceive the fact of cosmic harmony as exclusively due to the causes which the scientific train of reasoning assigns. But freely conceding this much, and an atheist may reply, that although the objections of his antagonist against this symbolic method of reasoning are undoubtedly valid, yet, from the nature of the case, this is the only method of scientific reasoning which is available. If, therefore, he expresses his obligations to his antagonist for pointing out a source of weakness in this method of reasoning—a source of weakness, be it observed, which renders it impossible for him to estimate the actual, as distinguished from the apparent, probability of the conclusion attained—this is all that he can be expected to do: he cannot be expected to abandon the only scientific method of reasoning available, in favour of a metaphysical method which only escapes the charge of symbolism by leaping with a single bound from a known cause (human intelligence) to the inference of an unknowable cause (Divine Intelligence). For the atheist may well point out that, however objectionable his scientific method of reasoning may be on account of the symbolism which it involves, it must at any rate be preferable to the metaphysical method, in that its symbols throughout refer to known causes.[1] With regard, then, to this stricture on the scientific method of reasoning, I conclude that although the caveat which it contains should never be lost sight of by atheists, it is not of sufficient cogency to justify theists in abandoning a scientific in favour of a metaphysical mode of reasoning.

How then does it fare with the other stricture, or the consideration that, " when the conclusion thus illegitimately [2] evolved is confronted with the fact of cosmic harmony which it professes to explain, we find it to be beyond the powers of human thought to conceive of such an effect as due to such a cause " ? The atheist may answer, in the first place, that a great deal here turns on the precise meaning which we assign to the word " conceive." For we have just seen that, by employing " symbolic conceptions," we *are* able to frame what we may term a *formal* conception of universal harmony as due to the persistence of force and the primary qualities of matter. That is to say, we have seen that such universal harmony as nature presents must be regarded as an effect of the collective operation of general laws ; and we have previously arrived

---

[1] It may be here observed that this quality of indefiniteness on the part of such reasoning is merely a practical outcome of the theoretical considerations adduced in Chapter V. For as we there saw that the ratio between the known and the unknown is in this case wholly indefinite, it follows that any symbols derived from the region of the known—even though such symbols be the highest generalities which the latter region affords—must be wholly indefinite when projected into the region of the unknown. Or rather let us say, that as the region of the unknown is but a progressive continuation of the region of the known, the determinate value of symbols of thought varies inversely as the distance—or, not improbably, as the square of the distance—from the sphere of the known at which they are applied.

[2] *i.e.*, illegitimate in a *relative* sense. The conclusion is legitimate enough in a *formal* sense, and as establishing a probability of some *unassignable* degree of value. But it would be illegitimate if this quality of indefiniteness were disregarded, and the conclusion supposed to possess the same character of actual probability as it has of formal definition.

at a formal conception of general laws as singly and collectively the product of self-evolution. Consequently, the word "conceive," as used in the theistic argument, must be taken to mean our ability to frame what we may term a *material* conception, or a representation in thought of the whole history of cosmic evolution, which representation shall be in some satisfactory degree intellectually realisable. Observing, then, this important difference between an inconceivability which arises from an impossibility of establishing relations in thought between certain *abstract* or *symbolic* conceptions, and an inconceivability which arises from a mere failure to realise in imagination the results which must follow among external relations if the symbolically conceivable combinations among them ever took place, an atheist may here argue as follows; and it does not appear that there is any legitimate escape from his reasonings.

'I first consider the undoubted fact that the existence of a Supreme Mind in nature is, scientifically considered, unnecessary; and, therefore, that the only reason we require to entertain the supposition of any such existence at all is, that the complexity of nature being so great, we are unable adequately to conceive of its self-evolution—notwithstanding our reason tells us plainly that, given a self-existing universe of force and matter, and such self-evolution becomes abstractedly possible. I then reflect that this is a negative and not a positive ground of belief. If the hypothesis of self-evolution is true, we should *à priori* expect that by the time evolution had advanced sufficiently far to admit of the production of a reasoning intelligence, the complexity of nature must be so great that the nascent reasoning powers would be completely baffled in their attempts to comprehend the various processes going on around them. This seems to be about the state of things which we now experience. Still, as reason advances more and more, we may expect, both from general *à priori* principles and from particular historical analogies, that more and more of the processes of nature will admit of being interpreted by reason, and that in proportion as our ability to *understand* the frame and the constitution of things progresses, so our ability to *conceive* of them as all naturally and necessarily evolved will likewise and concurrently progress. Thus, for example, how vast a number of the most intricate and delicate correlations in nature have been rendered at once intelligible and conceivably due to non-intelligent causes, by the discovery of a single principle in nature—the principle of natural selection.

'In the adverse argument, conceivability is again made the unconditional test of truth, just as it was in the argument against the possibility of matter thinking. We reject the hypothesis of self-evolution, not because it is the more remote one, but simply because we experience a subjective incapacity adequately to frame the requisite generalisations in thought, or to frame them with as much clearness as we could wish. Yet our reason tells us as plainly as it tells us any general truth which is too large to be presented in detail, that there is nothing in the nature of things themselves, as far as we can see, antagonistic to the supposition of their having been self-evolved. Only on the ground, therefore, of our own intellectual deficiencies; only because as yet, by the self-evolutionary hypothesis, the inner order does not completely answer to the outer order; only because the number and complexity of subjective relations have not yet been able to rival those of the objective relations producing them; only on this ground do we refuse to assent to the obvious deductions of our reason.[1]

---

[1] In order not to burden the text with details, I have presented these reflections in their most general terms. Thus, if it be granted that cosmic harmony results from the combined action of general laws, and that these laws are the necessary result of the primary qualities of force and matter, this the most general statement of the atheistic position includes all more special considerations as a genus includes its species; and therefore it would not signify, for the purposes of the atheistic argument, whether or not any such more special considerations are possible. Nevertheless, for the sake of completeness, I may here

'And here I may observe, further, that the presumption in favour of atheism which these deductions establish is considerably fortified by certain *à posteriori* considerations which we cannot afford to overlook. In particular, I reflect that, as a matter of fact, the theistic theory is born of highly suspicious parentage,—that Fetichism, or the crudest form of the theory of personal agency in

observe, that we are not wholly without indications in nature of the physical causation whereby the effect of cosmic harmony is produced. The universal tendency of motion to become rhythmical — itself, as Mr. Spencer was the first to show, a necessary consequence of the persistence of force—is, so to speak, a conservative tendency: it sets a premium against natural cataclysms. But a more important consideration is this, —that during the evolution of natural law in the way suggested in Chapter IV., as every newly evolved law came into existence it must have been, as it were, grafted on the stock of all pre-existing natural laws, and so would not enter the cosmic system as an element of confusion, but rather as an element of further progress. For instance, when, with the origin of organic nature, the law of natural selection entered upon the cosmos, it was grafted upon the pre-existing stock of other natural laws, and so combined within them in unity. And a little thought will show that it was impossible that it should do otherwise; for it was impossible that natural selection could ever produce organisms which would ever be able by their existence to conflict with the pre-existing system of astronomic or geologic laws; seeing that organisms, being a product of later evolution than these laws, would either have to be adapted to them or perish. And hence the new law of natural selection, which consists in so adapting organisms to the pre-existing laws that they must either conform to them or die. Now, I have chosen the case of natural selection, because, as alluded to in the text, it is the law of all others which is the most conspicuously effective in producing the harmonious complexity of nature. But the same kind of considerations may be seen to apply to most of the other general laws with which we are acquainted, particularly if we bear in mind that the general outcome of their united action as we observe it— the cosmic harmony on which so much stress is laid—is not *perfectly* harmonious. Cataclysms—whether it be the capture of an insect, or the ruin of a star—although events of comparatively rare occurrence if at any given time we take into account the total number of insects or the total number of stars, are events which nevertheless do occasionally happen. And the fact that even cataclysms take place in accordance with so-called natural law, serves but to emphasise the consideration on which we are engaged—viz., that the total result of the combined action of general laws is not such as to produce perfect order. Lastly, if the answer is made that human ideas of perfect order may not correspond with the highest ideal of such order, I observe that to make such an answer is merely to abandon the subject of discussion; for if a theist rests his argument on the basis of our human conception of order, he is not free to maintain his argument and at the same time to abandon its basis at whatever point the latter may be shown untenable.

external nature, admits of being easily traced to the laws of a primitive psychology; that the step from this to Polytheism is easy; and that the step from this to Monotheism is necessary. If it is objected to this view that it does not follow that because some theories of personal agency have proved themselves false, therefore all such theories must be so—I answer, Unquestionably not; but the above considerations are not adduced in order to *negative* the theistic theory: they are merely adduced to show that the human mind has hitherto undoubtedly exhibited an undue and a vicious tendency to interpret the objective processes of nature in terms of its own subjective processes; and as we can see quite well that the current theory of personal agency in nature, whether or not true, is a necessary outcome of intellectual evolution, I think that the fact of so abundant an historical analogy ought to be allowed to lend a certain degree of antecedent suspicion to this theory—although, of course, the suspicion is of a kind which would admit of immediate destruction before any satisfactory positive evidence in favour of the theory.[1]

'But what is 'the satisfactory positive evidence' that is offered me? Nothing, save an alleged subjective incapacity on the part of my opponent adequately to conceive of the fact of cosmic harmony as due to physical causation alone. Now I have already commented on the weakness of his position; but as my opponent will doubtless resort to the consideration that inconceivability of an opposite is, after all, the best criterion of truth which at any given stage of intellectual evolution is available, I will now conclude my overthrow by pointing out that, even if we take the argument from teleology in its widest

[1] [Since the above was written, the first volume of Mr. Spencer's "Sociology" has been published; and those who may not as yet have read the first half of that work are here strongly recommended to do so; for Mr. Spencer has there shown, in a more connected and conclusive manner than has ever been shown before, how strictly natural is the growth of all superstitious and religious—*i.e.*, of all the theories of personal agency in nature.—1878.]

possible sense—the argument, I mean, from the general order and beauty of nature, as well as the gross constituent part of it from design—even taking this argument in its widest sense and upon its own ground (which ground, I presume, it is now sufficiently obvious *can* only be that of the inconceivability of its negation), I will conclude my examination of this argument by showing that it is quite as inconceivable to predicate cosmic harmony an effect of Intelligence, as it is to predicate it an effect of Non-intelligence; and therefore that the argument from inconceivability admits of being turned with quite as terrible a force upon Theism as it can be made to exert upon Atheism.

'" In metaphysical controversy, many of the propositions propounded and accepted as quite believable are absolutely inconceivable. There is a perpetual confusing of actual ideas with what are nothing but pseud-ideas. No distinction is made between propositions that contain real thoughts and propositions that are only the forms of thoughts. A thinkable proposition is one of which the *two terms can be brought together in consciousness under the relation said to exist between them.* But very often, when the subject of a proposition has been thought of as something known, and when the predicate of a proposition has been thought of as something known, and when the relation alleged between them has been thought of as a known relation, it is supposed that the proposition itself has been thought. The thinking separately of the elements of a proposition is mistaken for the thinking of them in the combination which the proposition affirms. And hence it continually happens that propositions which cannot be rendered into thought at all are supposed to be not only thought but believed. The proposition that Evolution is caused by Mind is one of this nature. The two terms are separately intelligible; but they can be regarded in the relation of effect and cause only so long as no attempt is made to put them together in this relation.

'"The only thing which any one knows as Mind is the series of his own states of consciousness; and if he thinks of any mind other than his own, he can think of it only in terms derived from his own. If I am asked to frame a notion of Mind divested of all those structural traits under which alone I am conscious of mind in myself, I cannot do it. I know nothing of thought save as carried on in ideas originally traceable to the effects wrought by objects on me. A mental act is an unintelligible phrase if I am not to regard it as an act in which states of consciousness are severally known as like other states in the series that has gone by, and in which the relations between them are severally known as like past relations in the series. If, then, I have to conceive evolution as caused by an 'originating Mind,' I must conceive this Mind as having attributes akin to those of the only mind I know, and without which I cannot conceive mind at all.

'"I will not dwell on the many incongruities hence resulting, by asking how the 'originating Mind' is to be thought of as having states produced by things objective to it, as discriminating among these states, and classing them as like and unlike; and as preferring one objective result to another. I will simply ask, What happens if we ascribe to the 'originating Mind' the character absolutely essential to the conception of mind, that it consists of a series of states of consciousness? Put a series of states of consciousness as cause and the evolving universe as effect, and then endeavour to see the last as flowing from the first. I find it possible to imagine in some dim way a series of states of consciousness serving as antecedent to any one of the movements I see going on; for my own states of consciousness are often indirectly the antecedents to such movements. But how if I attempt to think of such a series as antecedent to *all* actions throughout the universe—to the motions of the multitudinous stars throughout space, to the revolutions of all their planets round them, to the gyrations of all these planets on their axes, to the infinitely multiplied physical processes going on in each of these suns and planets? I cannot think of a single series of states of consciousness as causing even the relatively small groups of actions going on over the earth's surface. I cannot think of it even as antecedent to all the various winds and the dissolving clouds they bear, to the currents of all the rivers, and the grinding actions of all the glaciers; still less can I think of it as antecedent to the infinity of processes simultaneously going on in all the plants that cover the globe, from scattered polar lichens to crowded tropical palms, and in all the millions of quadrupeds that roam among them, and the millions of millions of insects that buzz about them. Even a single small set of these multitudinous terrestrial changes I cannot conceive as antecedent a single series of states of consciousness—cannot, for instance, think of it as causing the hundred thousand breakers that are at this instant curling over on the shores of England. How, then, is it possible for me to conceive an 'originating Mind,' which I must represent to myself as a *single* series of states of consciousness, working the infinitely multiplied sets of changes *simultaneously* going on in worlds too numerous to count, dispersed throughout a space that baffles imagination?

'"If, to account for this infinitude of physical changes everywhere going on, 'Mind must be conceived as there' 'under the guise of simple Dynamics,' then the reply is, that, to be so conceived, Mind must be divested of all attributes by which it is distinguished; and that, when thus divested of its distinguishing attributes, the conception disappears—the word Mind stands for a blank. . . .

'"Clearly, therefore, the proposition that an 'originating Mind' is the cause of evolution is a proposition that can be entertained so long only as no attempt is made to unite in thought its two terms in the alleged relation. That it should be accepted as a matter of *faith* may be a defensible position, provided good cause is shown why it should be so accepted; but that it should be accepted as a matter of *understanding*—as a statement making the order of the universe comprehensible—is a quite indefensible position."'[1]

§ 47. We have now heard the pleading on both sides of the ultimate issue to which it is possible that the argument from teleology can ever be reduced. It therefore devolves on us very briefly to adjudicate upon the contending opinions. And this it is not difficult to do; for throughout the pleading on both sides I have been careful to exclude all arguments and considerations which are not logically valid. It is therefore impossible for me now to pass any criticisms on the pleading of either side which have not already been passed by the pleading of the other. But nevertheless, in my capacity of an impartial judge, I feel it desirable to conclude this chapter with a few general considerations.

In the first place, I think that the theist's antecedent objection to a scientific mode of reasoning on the score of its symbolism, may be regarded as fairly balanced by the atheist's antecedent objection to a metaphysical mode of reasoning on the score of its postulating an unknowable cause. And it must be allowed that the force of this antecedent objection is considerably increased by the reflection that the *kind* of unknowable cause which is thus postulated is that which the human mind has always shown an overweening tendency to postulate as a cause of natural phenomena.

I think, therefore, that neither disputant has the right to regard the *à priori* standing of his opponent's theory as much more suspicious than that of his own; for it is obvious that neither disputant has the means whereby to estimate the actual value of these antecedent objections.

[1] Herbert Spencer's Essays, vol. iii. pp. 246-249 (1874).

With regard, then, to the *à posteriori* evidence in favour of the rival theories, I think that the final test of their validity—*i.e.*, the inconceivability of their respective negations—fails equally in the case of both theories; for in the case of each theory any proposition which embodies it must itself contain an infinite, *i.e.*, an inconceivable—term. Thus, whether we speak of an Infinite Mind as the cause of evolution, or of evolution as due to an infinite duration of physical processes, we are alike open to the charge of employing unthinkable propositions.

Hence, two unthinkables are presented to our choice; one of which is an eternity of matter and of force,[1] and the other an Infinite Mind, so that in this respect again the two theories are tolerably parallel; and therefore, all that can be concluded with rigorous certainty upon the subject is, that neither theory has anything to gain as against the other from an appeal to the test of inconceivability.

Yet we have seen that this is a test than which none can be more ultimate. What then shall we say is the final outcome of this discussion concerning the rational standing of the teleological argument? The answer, I think, to this question is, that in strict reasoning the teleological argument, in its every shape, is inadequate to form a basis of Theism; or, in other words, that the

---

[1] This is the truly inconceivable element in the physical theory. As I have shown in the pleading on the side of Atheism, the supposed inconceivability of cosmic harmony being due to mindless forces, is not of such a kind as wholly refuses to be surmounted by symbolic conceptions of a sufficiently abstract character. But it is impossible, by the aid of any symbols, to gain a conception of an eternal existence. And I may here point out, that if Mind is said to be the cause of evolution, not only does the statement involve the inconceivable proposition that such a Mind must be infinite in respect of its powers of supervision, direction, &c.; but the statement also involves a necessary alternative between two additional inconceivable propositions—viz., either that such a Mind must have been eternal, or that it must have come into existence without a cause. In this respect, therefore, it would seem that the theory of Atheism has the advantage over that of Theism; for while the former theory is under the necessity of embodying only a single inconceivable term, the latter theory is under the necessity of embodying two such terms.

logical cogency of this argument is insufficient to justify a wholly impartial mind in accepting the theory of Theism on so insecure a foundation. Nevertheless, if the further question were directly put to me, 'After having heard the pleading both for and against the most refined expression of the argument from teleology, with what degree of strictly rational probability do you accredit it?'—I should reply as follows:—' The question which you put I take to be a question which it is wholly impossible to answer, and this for the simple reason that the degree of even rational probability may here legitimately vary with the character of the mind which contemplates it.' This statement, no doubt, sounds paradoxical; but I think it is justified by the following considerations. When we say that one proposition is more conceivable than another, we may mean either of two very different things, and this quite apart from the distinction previously drawn between symbolic conceptions and realisable conceptions. For we may mean that one of the two propositions presents terms which cannot possibly be rendered into thought at all in the relation which the proposition alleges to subsist between them; or we may mean that one of the two propositions presents terms in a relation which is more congruous with the habitual tenor of our thoughts than does the other proposition. Thus, as an example of the former usage, we may say, It is more conceivable that two and two should make four than that two and two should make five; and, as an example of the latter usage, we may say, It is more conceivable that a man should be able to walk than that he should be able to fly. Now, for the sake of distinction, I shall call the first of these usages the test of *absolute* inconceivability, and the second the test of *relative* inconceivability. Doubtless, when the word "inconceivability" is used in the sense of relative inconceivability, it is incorrectly used, unless it is qualified in some way; because, if used without qualification, there is danger of its being confused with inconceivability in its absolute sense. Nevertheless, if used with some qualifying epithet, it becomes quite unexceptionable. For the process of conception being in all cases the process of establishing relations in thought, we may properly say, It is relatively more conceivable that a man should walk than that a man should fly, since it is *more easy* to establish the necessary relations in thought in the case of the former than in the case of the latter proposition. The only difference, then, between what I have called absolute inconceivability and what I have called relative inconceivability consists in this—that while the latter admits of *degrees*, the former does not.[1]

[1] Mr. Herbert Spencer has treated of this subject in his memorable controversy with Mill on the "Universal Postulate" (see *Psychology*, § 427), and refuses to entertain the term "Inconceivable" as applicable to any propositions other than those wherein "the terms cannot, by any effort, be brought before consciousness in that relation which the proposition asserts between them." That is to say, he limits the term "Inconceivable" to that which is *absolutely* inconceivable; and he then proceeds to affirm that all propositions "which admit of being framed in thought, but which are so much at variance with experience, in which its terms have habitually been otherwise united, that its terms cannot be put in the alleged relation without effort," ought properly to be termed "*incredible*" propositions. Now I cannot see that the class "Incredible propositions" is, as this definition asserts, identical with the class which I have termed "Relatively inconceivable" propositions. For example, it is a familiar observation that, on looking at the setting sun, we experience an almost, if not quite, insuperable difficulty in *conceiving* the sun's apparent motion as due to our own actual motion, and yet we experience no difficulty in *believing* it. Conversely, I entertain but little difficulty in *conceiving*—i.e., imagining—a shark with a mammalian heart, and yet it would require extremely strong evidence to make me *believe* that such an animal exists. The truth appears to be that our language is deficient in terms whereby to distinguish between that which is wholly inconceivable from that which is with difficulty conceivable. This, it seems to me, was the principal reason of the dispute between Spencer and Mill above alluded to,—the former writer having always used the word "Inconceivable" in the sense of "Absolutely inconceivable," and the latter having apparently used it—in his *Logic* and elsewhere—in both senses. I have endeavoured to remedy this defect in the language by introducing the qualifying words, "Absolutely" and "Relatively," which, although not appropriate words, are the best that I am able to supply. The conceptive faculty of the individual having been determined by the experience of the race, that which is inconceivable by the intelligence of the race may be said to be inconceivable to the intelligence of the individual in an *absolute* sense; no effort on his part can enable him to sur-

With this distinction clearly understood, I may now proceed to observe that in everyday life we constantly apply the test of relative inconceivability as a test of truth. And in the vast majority of cases this test of relative inconceivability is, for all practical purposes, as valid a test of truth as is the test of absolute conceivability. For as every man is more or less in harmony with his environment, his habits of thought with regard to his environment are for the most part stereotyped correctly; so that the most ready and the most trustworthy gauge of probability that he has is an immediate appeal to consciousness as to whether he *feels* the probability. Thus every man learns for himself to endow his own sense of probability with a certain undefined but massive weight of authority. Now it is this test of relative conceivability which all men apply in varying degrees to the question of Theism. For if, from education and organised habits of thought, the probability in this matter appears to a man to incline in a certain direction, when this probability is called in question, the whole body of this organised system of thought rises in opposition to the questioning, and being individually conscious of this strong feeling of subjective opposition, the man declares the sceptical propositions to be more inconceivable to him than are the counter-propositions. And in so saying he is, of course, perfectly right. Hence I conceive that the acceptance or the rejection of metaphysical teleology as probable will depend entirely upon individual habits of thought. The test of absolute inconceivability making

---

mount the organically imposed conditions of his conceptive faculty. But that which is inconceivable merely to one individual or generation, while it is not inconceivable to the intelligence of the race, may properly be said to be inconceivable to the intelligence of that individual or generation only in a *relative* sense; apart from the special conditions to which the individual intelligence has been subjected, there is nothing in the conditions of human intelligence as such to prevent the thing from being conceived. [While this work has been passing through the press, I have found that Mr. G. H. Lewes has already employed the above terms in precisely the same sense as that which is above explained.—1878.]

equally for and against the doctrine of Theism, disputants are compelled to fall back on the test of relative inconceivability; and as the direction in which the more inconceivable proposition will here seem to lie will be determined by previous habits of thought, it follows that while to a theist metaphysical teleology will appear a probable argument, to an atheist it will appear an improbable one. Thus to a theist it will no doubt appear more conceivable that the Supreme Mind should be such that in some of its attributes it resembles the human mind, while in other of its attributes—among which he will place omnipresence, omnipotence, and directive agency—it transcends the human mind as greatly as the latter "transcends mechanical motion;" and therefore that although it is true, as a matter of logical terminology, that we ought to designate such an entity "Not mind" or "Blank," still, as a matter of psychology, we may come nearer to the truth by assimilating in thought this entity with the nearest analogies which experience supplies, than by assimilating it in thought with any other entity—such as force or matter—which are felt to be in all likelihood still more remote from it in nature. On the other hand, to an atheist it will no doubt appear more conceivable, because more simple, to accept the dogma of an eternal self-existence of something which we call force and matter, and with this dogma to accept the implication of a necessary self-evolution of cosmic harmony, than to resort to the additional and no less inconceivable supposition of a self-existing Agent which must be regarded both as Mind and as Not-mind at the same time. But in both cases, in whatever degree this test of relative inconceivability of a negative is held by the disputants to be valid in solving the problem of Theism, in that degree is each man entitled to his respective estimate of the probability in question. And thus we arrive at the judgment that the rational probability of Theism legitimately varies with the character of the mind which contemplates it. For, as the test of absolute inconceivability is equally annihilative in whichever direction it is applied, the test of relative inconceivability is the only one that remains; and as the formal conditions of a metaphysical teleology are undoubtedly present on the one hand, and the formal conditions of a physical explanation of cosmic harmony are no less undoubtedly present on the other hand, it follows that a theist and an atheist have an equal right to employ this test of relative inconceivability. And as there is no more ultimate court of appeal whereby to decide the question than the universe as a whole, each man has here an equal argumentative right to abide by the decision which that court awards *to him individually*—to accept whatever probability the sum-total of phenomena appears to present to his particular understanding. And it is needless to say that experience shows, even among well-informed and accurate reasoners, how large an allowance must thus be made for personal equations. To some men the facts of external nature seem to proclaim a God with clarion voice, while to other men the same facts bring no whisper of such a message. All, therefore, that a logician can here do is to remark, that the individuals in each class—provided they bear in mind the strictly *relative* character of their belief—have a similar right to be regarded as holding a rational creed: the grounds of belief in this case logically vary with the natural disposition and the subsequent training of different minds.[1]

It only remains to show that disputants on either side

---

[1] I should here like to have added some consideration on Sir W. Hamilton's remarks concerning the effect of training upon the mind in this connection; but, to avoid being tedious, I shall condense what I have to say into a few sentences. What Hamilton maintains is very true, viz., that the study of classics, moral and mental philosophy, &c., renders the mind more capable of believing in a God than does the study of physical science. The question, however, is, Which class of studies ought to be considered the more authoritative in this matter? I certainly cannot see what title classics, history, political economy, &c., have to be regarded at all; and although the mental and moral sciences have doubtless a better claim, still I think they must be largely subordinate to those sciences which deal with the whole domain of nature besides.

are apt to endow this test of relative inconceivability with far more than its real logical worth. Being accustomed to apply this test of truth in daily life, and there finding it a trustworthy test, most men are apt to forget that its value as a test must clearly diminish in proportion to the distance from experience at which it is applied. This, indeed, we saw to be the case even with the test of absolute inconceivability (see Chapter V.), but much more must it be the case with this test of relative inconceivability. For, without comment, it is manifest that our acquired sense of probability, as distinguished from our innate sense of possibility, with regard to any particular question of a transcendental nature, cannot be at all comparable with its value in the case of ordinary questions, with respect to which our sense of probability is being always rectified by external facts. Although, therefore, it is true that both those who reject and those who retain a belief in Theism on grounds of relative conceivability are equally entitled to be regarded as displaying a rational attitude of mind, in whatever degree either party considers their belief as of a higher validity than the grounds of psychology from which it takes its rise, in that degree must the members of that party be deemed irrational. In other words, not only must a man be careful not to confuse the test of relative inconceivability with that of absolute conceivability—not to suppose that his sense of probability in this matter is determined by an innate psychological inability to conceive a proposition, when in reality it is only determined by the difficulty of dissociating ideas which have long been habitually associated;—but he must also be careful to remember that the test of relative inconceivability in this matter is only

---

Further, I should say that there is no very strong *affirmative* influence created on the mind in this respect by any class of studies; and that the only reason why we so generally find Theism and classics, &c., united, is because we so seldom find classics, &c., and physical science united; the *negative* influence of the latter, in the case of classical minds, being therefore generally absent.

valid as justifying a belief of the most diffident possible kind.

And from this the practical deduction is—tolerance. Let no man think that he has any argumentative right to expect that the mere subjective habit or tone of his own mind should exert any influence on that of his fellow; but rather let him always remember that the only legitimate weapons of his intellectual warfare are those the *material* of which is derived from the external world, and only the *form* of which is due to the forging process of his own mind. And if in battle such weapons seem to be unduly blunted on the hardened armoury of traditional beliefs, or on the no less hardened armoury of confirmed scepticism, let him remember further that he must not too confidently infer that the fault does not lie in the character of his own weapons. To drop the figure, let none of us forget in how much need we all stand of this caution:—Knowing how greatly the value of arguments is affected, even to the most impartial among us, by the frame of mind in which we regard them, let all of us be jealously careful not to over-estimate the certainty that our frame or habit of mind is actually superior to that of our neighbour. And, in conclusion, it is surely needless to insist on the yet greater need there is for most of us to bear in mind this further caution:—Knowing with what great subjective opposition arguments are met when they conflict with our established modes of thought, let us all be jealously careful to guard the sanctuary of our judgment from the polluting tyranny of habit.

CHAPTER VII.

GENERAL SUMMARY AND CONCLUSIONS.

§ 48. Our analysis is now at an end, and a very few words will here suffice to convey an epitomised recollection of the numerous facts and conclusions which we have found it necessary to contemplate. We first disposed of the conspicuously absurd supposition that the origin of things, or the mystery of existence, admits of being explained by the theory of Theism in any further degree than by the theory of Atheism. Next it was shown that the argument " Our heart requires a God " is invalid, seeing that such a subjective necessity, even if made out, could not be sufficient to prove—or even to render probable—an objective existence. And with regard to the further argument that the fact of our theistic aspirations point to God as to their explanatory cause, it became necessary to observe that the argument could only be admissible after the possibility of the operation of natural causes had been excluded. Similarly the argument from the supposed intuitive necessity of individual thought was found to be untenable, first, because, even if the supposed necessity were a real one, it would only possess an individual applicability; and second, that, as a matter of fact, it is extremely improbable that the supposed necessity is a real necessity even for the individual who asserts it, while it is absolutely certain that it is not such to the vast majority of the race. The argument from the general consent of mankind, being so obviously fallacious both as to facts and principles, was passed over without

GENERAL SUMMARY AND CONCLUSIONS. 103

comment; while the argument from a first cause was found to involve a logical suicide. Lastly, the argument that, as human volition is a cause in nature, therefore all causation is probably volitional in character, was shown to consist in a stretch of inference so outrageous that the argument had to be pronounced worthless.

Proceeding next to examine the less superficial arguments in favour of Theism, it was first shown that the syllogism, All known minds are caused by an unknown mind; our mind is a known mind; therefore our mind is caused by an unknown mind,—is a syllogism that is inadmissible for two reasons. In the first place, "it does not account for mind (in the abstract) to refer it to a prior mind for its origin;" and therefore, although the hypothesis, if admitted, would be *an* explanation of *known* mind, it is useless as an argument for the existence of the unknown mind, the assumption of which forms the basis of that explanation. Again, in the next place, if it be said that mind is so far an entity *sui generis* that it must be either self-existing or caused by another mind, there is no assignable warrant for the assertion. And this is the second objection to the above syllogism; for anything within the whole range of the possible may, for aught that we can tell, be competent to produce a self-conscious intelligence. Thus an objector to the above syllogism need not hold any theory of things at all; but even as opposed to the definite theory of materialism, the above syllogism has not so valid an argumentative basis to stand upon. We know that what we call matter and force are to all appearance eternal, while we have no corresponding evidence of a "mind that is even apparently eternal." Further, within experience mind is invariably associated with highly differentiated collocations of matter and distributions of force, and many facts go to prove, and none to negative, the conclusion that the grade of intelligence invariably depends upon, or at least is associated with, a corresponding grade of cerebral development. There is thus both a qualitative and a quantitative relation between intelligence and cerebral organisation. And if it is said that matter and motion cannot produce consciousness because it is inconceivable that they should, we have seen at some length that this is no conclusive consideration as applied to a subject of a confessedly transcendental nature, and that in the present case it is particularly inconclusive, because, as it is speculatively certain that the substance of mind must be unknowable, it seems *à priori* probable that, whatever is the cause of the unknowable reality, this cause should be more difficult to render into thought in that relation than would some other hypothetical substance which is imagined as more akin to mind. And if it is said that the *more* conceivable cause is the *more* probable cause, we have seen that it is in this case impossible to estimate the validity of the remark. Lastly, the statement that the cause must contain actually all that its effects can contain, was seen to be inadmissible in logic and contradicted by everyday experience; while the argument from the supposed freedom of the will and the existence of the moral sense was negatived both deductively by the theory of evolution, and inductively by the doctrine of utilitarianism. On the whole, then, with regard to the argument from the existence of the human mind, we were compelled to decide that it is destitute of any assignable weight, there being nothing more to lead to the conclusion that our mind has been caused by another mind, than to the conclusion that it has been caused by anything else whatsoever.

With regard to the argument from Design, it was observed that Mill's presentation of it is merely a resuscitation of the argument as presented by Paley, Bell, and Chalmers. And indeed we saw that the first-named writer treated this whole subject with a feebleness and inaccuracy very surprising in him; for while he has failed to assign anything like due weight to the inductive evidence of organic evolution, he did not hesitate to rush into a supernatural explanation of biological phenomena. Moreover, he has failed signally in his *analysis* of the Design argument, seeing that, in common with all previous writers, he failed to observe that it is utterly impossible for us to know the relations in which the supposed Designer stands to the Designed,—much less to argue from the fact that the Supreme Mind, even supposing it to exist, caused the observable products by any particular intellectual *process*. In other words, all advocates of the Design argument have failed to perceive that, even if we grant nature to be due to a creating Mind, still we have no shadow of a right to conclude that this Mind can only have exerted its creative power by means of such and such cogitative operations. How absurd, therefore, must it be to raise the supposed evidence of such cogitative operations into evidences of the existence of a creating Mind! If a theist retorts that it is, after all, of very little importance whether or not we are able to divine the *methods* of creation, so long as the *facts* are there to attest that, *in some way or other*, the observable phenomena of nature must be due to Intelligence of some kind as their ultimate cause, then I am the first to endorse this remark. It has always appeared to me one of the most unaccountable things in the history of speculation that so many competent writers can have insisted upon *Design* as an argument for Theism, when they must all have known perfectly well that they have no means of ascertaining the subjective psychology of that Supreme Mind whose existence the argument is adduced to demonstrate. The truth is, that the argument from teleology must, and can only, rest upon the observable *facts* of nature, without reference to the intellectual *processes* by which these facts may be supposed to have been accomplished. But, looking to the "present state of our knowledge," this is merely to change the teleological argument from its gross Paleyerian form, into the argument from the ubiquitous operation of general laws. And we saw that this transformation is now a rational necessity. How far the great principle of natural selection may have been instrumental in the evolution of organic forms, is not here, as Mill erroneously imagined, the question; the question is simply as to whether we are to accept the theory of special creation or the theory of organic evolution. And forasmuch as no competent judge at the present time can hesitate for one moment in answering this question, the argument from a proximate teleology must be regarded as no longer having any rational existence.

How then does it fare with the last of the arguments—the argument from an ultimate teleology? Doubtless at first sight this argument seems a very powerful one, inasmuch as it is a generic argument, which embraces not only biological phenomena, but all the phenomena of the universe. But nevertheless we are constrained to acknowledge that its apparent power dwindles to nothing in view of the indisputable fact that, if force and matter have been eternal, all and every natural law must have resulted by way of necessary consequence. It will be remembered that I dwelt at considerable length and with much earnestness upon this truth, not only because of its enormous importance in its bearing upon our subject, but also because no one has hitherto considered it in that relation.

The next step, however, was to mitigate the severity of the conclusion that was liable to be formed upon the utter and hopeless collapse of all the possible arguments in favour of Theism. Having fully demonstrated that there is no shadow of a positive argument in support of the theistic theory, there arose the danger that some persons might erroneously conclude that for this reason the theistic theory must be untrue. It therefore became necessary to point out, that although, as far as we can see, nature does not require an Intelligent Cause to account for any of her phenomena, yet it is possible that, if we could see farther, we should see that nature could not be what she is unless she had owed her existence to an Intelligent Cause. Or, in other words, the probability there is that an Intelligent Cause is unnecessary to explain any of the phenomena of nature, is only equal to the probability there is that the doctrine of the persistence of force is everywhere and eternally true.

As a final step in our analysis, therefore, we altogether quitted the region of experience, and ignoring even the very foundations of science, and so all the most certain of relative truths, we carried the discussion into the transcendental region of purely formal considerations. And here we laid down the canon, "that the value of any probability, in its last analysis, is determined by the number, the importance, and the definiteness of the relations known, as compared with those of the relations unknown;" and, consequently, that in cases where the unknown relations are more numerous, more important, or more indefinite than are the known relations, the value of our inference varies inversely as the difference in these respects between the relations compared. From which canon it followed, that as the problem of Theism is the most ultimate of all problems, and so contains in its unknown relations all that is to man unknown and unknowable, these relations must be pronounced the most indefinite of all relations that it is possible for man to contemplate; and, consequently, that although we have here the entire range of experience from which to argue, we are unable to estimate the real value of any argument whatsoever. The unknown relations in our attempted induction being wholly indefinite, both in respect of their number and importance, as compared with the known relations, it is impossible for us to determine any definite probability either for or against the being of a God. Therefore, although it is true that, so far as human science can penetrate or human thought infer, we can perceive no evidence of God, yet we have no right on this account to conclude that there is no God. The probability, therefore, that nature is devoid of Deity, while it is of the strongest kind if regarded scientifically—amounting, in fact, to a scientific demonstration,—is nevertheless wholly worthless if regarded logically. Notwithstanding it is as true as is the fundamental basis of all science and of all experience that, if there is a God, his existence, considered as a cause of the universe, is superfluous, it may nevertheless be true that, if there had never been a God, the universe could never have existed.

Hence these formal considerations proved conclusively that, no matter how great the probability of Atheism might appear to be in a relative sense, we have no means of estimating such probability in an absolute sense. From which position there emerged the possibility of another argument in favour of Theism—or rather let us say, of a reappearance of the teleological argument in another form. For it may be said, seeing that these formal considerations exclude legitimate reasoning either for or against Deity in an absolute sense, while they do not exclude such reasoning in a relative sense, if there yet remain any theistic deductions which may properly be drawn from experience, these may now be adduced to balance the atheistic deductions from the persistence of force. For although the latter deductions have clearly shown the existence of Deity to be superfluous in a scientific sense, the formal considerations in question have no less clearly opened up beyond the sphere of science a possible *locus* for the existence of Deity; so that if there are any facts supplied by experience for which the atheistic deductions appear insufficient to account, we are still free to account for them in a relative sense by the hypothesis of Theism. And, it may be urged, we do find such an unexplained residuum in the correlation of general laws in the production of cosmic harmony. It signifies nothing, the argument may run, that we are unable to conceive the methods whereby the supposed Mind operates in producing cosmic harmony; nor does it signify that its operation must now be relegated to a super-scientific province. What does signify is that, taking a general view of nature, we find it impossible to conceive of the extent and variety of her harmonious processes as other than products of intelligent causation. Now this sublimated form of the teleological argument, it will be remembered, I denoted a metaphysical teleology, in order sharply to distinguish it from all previous forms of that argument, which, in contradistinction I denoted scientific teleologies. And the distinction, it will be remembered, consisted in this—that while all previous forms of teleology, by resting on a basis which was not beyond the possible reach of science, laid themselves open to the possibility of scientific refutation, the metaphysical system of teleology, by resting on a basis which is clearly beyond the possible reach of science, can never be susceptible of scientific refutation. And that this metaphysical system of teleology does rest on such a basis is indisputable; for while it accepts the most ultimate truths of which science can ever be cognisant—viz., the persistence of force and the consequently necessary genesis of natural law,—it nevertheless maintains that the necessity of regarding Mind as the ultimate cause of things is not on this account removed; and, therefore, that if science now requires the operation of a Supreme Mind to be posited in a super-scientific sphere, then in a super-scientific sphere it ought to be posited. No doubt this hypothesis at first sight seems gratuitous, seeing that, so far as science can penetrate, there is no need of any such hypothesis at all—cosmic harmony resulting as a physically necessary consequence from the combined action of natural laws, which in turn result as a physically necessary consequence of the persistence of force and the primary qualities of matter. But although it is thus indisputably true that metaphysical teleology is wholly gratuitous if considered scientifically, it may not be true that it is wholly gratuitous if considered psychologically. In other words, if it is more conceivable that Mind should be the ultimate cause of cosmic harmony than that the persistence of force should be so, then it is not irrational to accept the more conceivable hypothesis in preference to the less conceivable one, provided that the choice is made with the diffidence which is required by the considerations adduced in Chapter V.

I conclude, therefore, that the hypothesis of metaphysical teleology, although in a physical sense gratuitous, may be in a psychological sense legitimate. But as against the fundamental position on which alone this argument can rest—viz., the position that the fundamental postulate of Atheism is more *inconceivable* than is the fundamental postulate of Theism—we have seen two important objections to lie.

For, in the first place, the sense in which the word "inconceivable" is here used is that of the impossibility of framing *realisable* relations in the thought; not that of the impossibility of framing *abstract* relations in thought. In the same sense, though in a lower degree, it is true that the complexity of the human organisation and its functions is inconceivable; but in this sense the word "inconceivable" has much less weight in an argument than it has in its true sense. And, without waiting again to dispute (as we did in the case of the speculative standing of Materialism) how far even the genuine test of inconceivability ought to be allowed to make against an inference which there is a body of scientific evidence to substantiate, we went on to the second objection against this fundamental position of metaphysical teleology. This objection, it will be remembered, was, that it is as impossible to conceive of cosmic harmony as an effect of Mind, as it is to conceive of it as an effect of mindless evolution. The argument from inconceivability, therefore, admits of being turned with quite as terrible an effect on Theism, as it can possibly be made to exert on Atheism.

Hence this more refined form of teleology which we

are considering, and which we saw to be the last of the possible arguments in favour of Theism, is met on its own ground by a very crushing opposition: by its metaphysical character it has escaped the opposition of physical science, only to encounter a new opposition in the region of pure psychology to which it fled. As a conclusion to our whole inquiry, therefore, it devolved on us to determine the relative magnitudes of these opposing forces. And in doing this we first observed that, if the supporters of metaphysical teleology objected *à priori* to the method whereby the genesis of natural law was deduced from the datum of the persistence of force, in that this method involved an unrestricted use of illegitimate symbolic conceptions; then it is no less open to an atheist to object *à priori* to the method whereby a directing Mind was inferred from the datum of cosmic harmony, in that this method involved the postulation of an unknowable cause,—and this of a character which the whole history of human thought has proved the human mind to exhibit an overweening tendency to postulate as the cause of natural phenomena. On these grounds, therefore, I concluded that, so far as their respective standing *à priori* is concerned, both theories may be regarded as about equally suspicious. And similar with regard to their standing *à posteriori;* for as both theories require to embody at least one infinite term, they must each alike be pronounced absolutely inconceivable. But, finally, if the question were put to me which of the two theories I regarded as the more rational, I observed that this is a question which no one man can answer for another. For as the test of absolute inconceivability is equally destructive of both theories, if a man wishes to choose between them, his choice can only be determined by what I have designated relative inconceivability—*i.e.*, in accordance with the verdict given by his individual sense of probability as determined by his previous habits of thought. And forasmuch as the test of relative inconceivability may be held in this matter legitimately to vary with the character of the mind which applies it, the strictly rational probability of the question to which it is applied varies in like manner. Or, otherwise presented, the only alternative for any man in this matter is either to discipline himself into an attitude of pure scepticism, and thus to refuse in thought to entertain either a probability or an improbability concerning the existence of a God; or else to incline in thought towards an affirmation or a negation of God, according as his previous habits of thought have rendered such an inclination more facile in the one direction than in the other. And although, under such circumstances, I should consider that man the more rational who carefully suspended his judgment, I conclude that if this course is departed from, neither the metaphysical teleologist nor the scientific atheist has any perceptible advantage over the other in respect of rationality. For as the formal conditions of a metaphysical teleology are undoubtedly present on the one hand, and the formal conditions of a speculative atheism are as undoubtedly present on the other, there is thus in both cases a logical vacuum supplied wherein the pendulum of thought is free to swing in whichever direction it may be made to swing by the momentum of preconceived ideas.

§ 49. Such is the outcome of our investigation, and considering the abstract nature of the subject, the immense divergence of opinion which at the present time is manifested with regard to it, as well as the confusing amount of good, bad, and indifferent literature on both sides of the controversy which is extant;—considering these things, I do not think that the result of our inquiry can be justly complained of on the score of its lacking precision. At a time like the present, when traditional beliefs respecting Theism are so generally accepted and so commonly concluded, as a matter of course, to have a large and valid basis of induction whereon to rest, I cannot but feel that a perusal of this short essay, by showing how very concise the scientific *status* of the subject really is, will do more to settle the minds of most readers as to the exact standing at the present time of all the probabilities of the question, than could a perusal of all the rest of the literature upon this subject. And, looking to the present condition of speculative philosophy, I regard it as of the utmost importance to have clearly shown that the advance of science has now entitled us to assert, without the least hesitation, that the hypothesis of Mind in nature is as certainly superfluous to account for any of the phenomena of nature, as the scientific doctrine of the persistence of force and the indestructibility of matter is certainly true.

On the other hand, if any one is inclined to complain that the logical aspect of the question has not proved itself so unequivocally definite as has the scientific, I must ask him to consider that, in any matter which does not admit of actual demonstration, some margin must of necessity be left for variations of individual opinion. And, if he bears this consideration in mind, I feel sure that he cannot properly complain of my not having done my utmost in this case to define as sharply as possible the character and the limits of this margin.

§ 54. And now, in conclusion, I feel it is desirable to state that any antecedent bias with regard to Theism which I individually possess is unquestionably on the side of traditional beliefs. It is therefore with the utmost sorrow that I find myself compelled to accept the conclusions here worked out; and nothing would have induced me to publish them, save the strength of my conviction that it is the duty of every member of society to give his fellows the benefit of his labours for whatever they may be worth. Just as I am confident that truth must in the end be the most profitable for the race, so I am persuaded that every individual endeavour to attain it, provided only that such endeavour is unbiassed and sincere, ought without hesitation to be made the common property of all men, no matter in what direction the results of its promulgation may appear to tend. And so far as the ruination of individual happiness is concerned, no one can have a more lively perception than myself of the possibly disastrous tendency of my work. So far as I am individually concerned, the result of this analysis has been to show that, whether I regard the problem of Theism on the lower plane of strictly relative probability, or on the higher plane of purely formal considerations, it equally becomes my obvious duty to stifle all belief of the kind which I conceive to be the noblest, and to discipline my intellect with regard to this matter into an attitude of the purest scepticism. And forasmuch as I am far from being able to agree with those who affirm that the twilight doctrine of the "new faith" is a desirable substitute for the waning splendour of "the old," I am not ashamed to confess that with this virtual negation of God the universe to me has lost its soul of loveliness; and although from henceforth the precept to "work while it is day" will doubtless but gain an intensified force from the terribly intensified meaning of the words that "the night cometh when no man can work," yet when at times I think, as think at times I must, of the appalling contrast between the hallowed glory of that creed which once was mine, and the lonely mystery of existence as now I find it,—at such times I shall ever feel it impossible to avoid the sharpest pang of which my nature is susceptible. For whether it be due to my intelligence not being sufficiently advanced to meet the requirements of the age, or whether it be due to the memory of those sacred associations which to me at least were the sweetest that life has given, I cannot but feel that for me, and for others who think as I do, there is a dreadful truth in those words of Hamilton,—Philosophy having become a meditation, not merely of death, but of annihilation, the precept *know thyself* has become transformed into the terrific oracle to Œdipus—

"Mayest thou ne'er know the truth of what thou art."

APPENDIX

AND

SUPPLEMENTARY ESSAYS.

APPENDIX.

A CRITICAL EXPOSITION OF A FALLACY IN LOCKE'S USE OF THE ARGUMENT AGAINST THE POSSIBILITY OF MATTER THINKING ON GROUNDS OF ITS BEING INCONCEIVABLE THAT IT SHOULD.

LEST it should be thought that I am doing injustice to the views of this illustrious theist, I here quote his own words:—" We have the ideas of matter and thinking, but possibly shall never be able to know whether any mere material being thinks or no, it being impossible for us, by the contemplation of our own ideas, without revelation, to discover whether omnipotency has not given to some systems of matter fitly disposed a power to perceive and think, or else joined and fixed to matter so disposed a thinking immaterial substance; it being, in respect of our notions, not much more remote from our comprehension to conceive that God can, if He pleases, superadd to matter a faculty of thinking, than that He should superadd to it another substance with a faculty of thinking; since we know not wherein thinking consists, nor to what sort of substance the Almighty has been pleased to give that power, which cannot be in any created being, but merely by the good pleasure and bounty of the Creator. For I see no contradiction in it that the first eternal thinking being should, if he pleased, give to certain systems of created senseless matter, put together as he thinks fit, some degrees of sense, perception, and thought: though, as I think, I have proved, lib: iv., ch. 10 and 14, &c., it is no less than a contradiction to suppose matter (which is evidently in its own nature void of sense and thought) should be that eternal first-thinking being. What certainty of knowledge can any one have that some perceptions, such as, *e.g.*, pleasure and pain, should not be in some bodies themselves, after a certain manner modified and moved, as well as that they should be in an immaterial substance upon the motion of the parts of body? Body, as far as we can conceive, being able only to strike and affect body; and motion, according to the utmost reach of our ideas, being able to produce nothing but motion: so that when we allow it to produce pleasure or pain, or the idea of a colour or sound, we are fain to quit our reason, go beyond our ideas, and attribute it wholly to the good pleasure of our Maker. For since we must allow He has annexed effects to motion which we can no way conceive motion able to produce, what reason have we to conclude that He could not order them as well to be produced in a subject we cannot conceive capable of them, as well as in a subject we cannot conceive the motion of matter can any way operate upon? I say not this, that I would any way lessen the belief of the soul's immateriality, &c. . . . It is a point which seems to me to be put out of the reach of our knowledge; and he who will give himself leave to consider freely, and look into the dark and intricate part of each hypothesis, will scarce find his reason able to determine him fixedly for or against the soul's materiality. Since on which side soever he views it, either as an unextended substance or as a thinking extended matter, the difficulty to conceive either will, whilst either alone is in his thoughts, still drive him to the contrary side. An unfair way which some men take with themselves, who, because of the inconceivableness of something they find in one, throw themselves violently into the contrary hypothesis, though altogether as unintelligible to an unbiassed understanding."

This passage, I do not hesitate to say, is one of the

most remarkable in the whole range of philosophical literature, in respect of showing how even the strongest and most candid intellect may have its reasoning faculty impaired by the force of a preformed conviction. Here we have a mind of unsurpassed penetration and candour, which has left us side by side two parallel trains of reasoning. In the one, the object is to show that the author's preformed conviction as to the being of a God is justifiable on grounds of reason; in the other, the object is to show that, granting the existence of a God, and it is not impossible that he may have endowed matter with the faculty of thinking. Now, in the former train of reasoning, the whole proof rests entirely upon the fact that "it is impossible to conceive that ever bare incogitative matter should produce a thinking intelligent being." Clearly, if this proposition is true, it must destroy one or other of the trains of reasoning; for it is common to them both, and in one of them it is made the sole ground for concluding that matter cannot think, while in the other it is made compatible with the supposition that matter may think. This extraordinary inconsistency no doubt arose from the fact that the author was antecedently persuaded of the existence of an *Omnipotent* Mind, and having been long accustomed in his intellectual symbols to regard it presumptuous in him to impose any limitations on this almighty power, when he asked himself whether it would be possible for this almighty power, if it so willed, to endow matter with the faculty of thinking, he argued that it might be possible, notwithstanding his being unable to conceive the possibility. But when he banished from his mind the idea of this personal and almighty power, and with that idea banished all its associations, he then felt that he had a right to argue more freely, and forthwith made his conceptive faculty a test of abstract possibility. Yet *the sum total of abstract possibility, in relation to him, must have been the same in the two cases ;* so that in whichever of the two trains of reasoning his argument was sound, in the other it must certainly have been null.

We may well feel amazed that so able a thinker can have fallen into so obvious an error, and afterwards have persisted in it through pages and pages of his work. It will be instructive, however, to those who rely upon Locke's exposition of the argument from Inconceivability to see how effectually he has himself destroyed it. For this purpose, therefore, I shall make some further quotations from the same train of reasoning. The statement of Locke's opinion that the Almighty could endow matter with the faculty of thinking if He so willed, called down some remonstrances and rebukes from the then Bishop of Worcester. Locke's reply was a very lengthy one, and from it the following extracts are taken. I merely request the reader throughout to substitute for the words God, Creator, Almighty, Omnipotency, &c., the words *Summum genus* of Possibility.

"But it is further urged that we cannot conceive how matter can think. I grant it, but to argue from thence that God therefore cannot give to matter a faculty of thinking is to say God's omnipotency is limited to a narrow compass because man's understanding is so, and brings down God's infinite power to the size of our capacities. . . .

"If God can give no power to any parts of matter but what men can account for from the essence of matter in general; if all such qualities and properties must destroy the essence, or change the essential properties of matter, which are to our conceptions above it, and we cannot conceive to be the natural consequence of that essence; it is plain that the essence of matter is destroyed, and its essential properties changed, in most of the sensible parts of this our system. For it is visible that all the planets have revolutions about certain remote centres, which I would have any one explain or make conceivable by the bare essence, or natural powers depending on the essence of matter in general, without something added to that essence which we cannot conceive; for the moving of matter in a crooked line, or the attraction of matter by matter, is all that can be said in the case; either of which it is above our reach to derive from the essence of matter or body in general, though one of these two must unavoidably be allowed to be superadded, in this instance, to the essence of matter in general. The omnipotent Creator advised not with us in the making of the world, and His ways are not the less excellent because they are past finding out. . . .

"In all such cases, the superinducement of greater perfections and nobler qualities destroys nothing of the essence or perfections that were there before, unless there can be showed a manifest repugnancy between them; but all the proof offered for that is only that we cannot conceive how matter, without such superadded perfections, can produce such effects; which is, in truth, no more than to say matter in general, or every part of matter, as matter, has them not, but is no reason to prove that God, if He pleases, cannot superadd them to some parts of matter, unless it can be proved to be a contradiction that God should give to some parts of matter qualities and perfections which matter in general has not, though we cannot conceive how matter is invested with them, or how it operates by virtue of those new endowments; nor is it to be wondered that we cannot, whilst we limit all its operations to those qualities it had before, and would explain them by the known properties of matter in general, without any such induced perfections. For if this be a right rule of reasoning, to deny a thing to be because we cannot conceive the manner how it comes to be, I shall desire them who use it to stick to this rule, and see what work it will make both in divinity as well as philosophy, and whether they can advance anything more in favour of scepticism.

"For to keep within the present subject of the power of thinking and self-motion bestowed by omnipotent power in some parts of matter: the objection to this is, I cannot conceive how matter should think. What is the consequence? Ergo, God cannot give it a power to think. Let this stand for a good reason, and then proceed in other cases by the same.

"You cannot conceive how matter can attract matter at any distance, much less at the distance of 1,000,000 miles; ergo, God cannot give it such a power: you cannot conceive how matter should feel or move itself, or affect any material being, or be moved by it; ergo, God cannot give it such powers: which is in effect to deny gravity, and the revolution of the planets about the sun; to make brutes mere machines, without sense or spontaneous motion; and to allow man neither sense nor voluntary motion.

"Let us apply this rule one degree further. You cannot conceive how an extended solid substance should think, therefore God cannot make it think: can you conceive how your own soul or any substance thinks? You find, indeed, that you do think, and so do I; but I want to be told how the action of thinking is performed: this, I confess, is beyond my conception; and I would be glad any one who conceives it would explain it to me.

"God, I find, has given me this faculty; and since I cannot but be convinced of His power in this instance, which, though I every moment experience in myself, yet I cannot conceive the manner of, what would it be less than an insolent absurdity to deny His power in other like cases, only for this reason, because I cannot conceive the manner how? . . .

"That Omnipotency cannot make a substance to be solid and not solid at the same time, I think with due reverence [diffidence?[1]] we may say; but that a solid substance may not have qualities, perfections, and powers,

---

[1] The qualities named are only known in a relative sense, and therefore the apparent contradiction may be destitute of meaning in an absolute sense.

which have no natural or visibly necessary connection with solidity and extension, is too much for us (who are but of yesterday, and know nothing) to be positive in.

"If God cannot join things together by connections inconceivable to us, we must deny even the consistency and being of matter itself; since every particle of it having some bulk, has its parts connected by ways inconceivable to us. So that all the difficulties that are raised against the thinking of matter, from our ignorance or narrow conceptions, stand not at all in the way of the power of God, if He pleases to ordain it so; nor prove anything against His having actually endowed some parcels of matter, so disposed as He thinks fit, with a faculty of thinking, till it can be shown that it contains a contradiction to suppose it.

"Though to me sensation be comprehended under thinking in general, in the foregoing discourse I have spoke of sense in brutes as distinct from thinking; because your lordship, as I remember, speaks of sense in brutes. But here I take liberty to observe, that if your lordship allows brutes to have sensation, it will follow, either that God can and doth give to some parcels of matter a power of perception and thinking, or that all animals have immaterial, and consequently, according to your lordship, immortal souls, as well as men; and to say that fleas and mites, &c., have immortal souls as well as men, will possibly be looked on as going a great way to serve an hypothesis. . . .

"It is true, I say, 'That bodies operate by impulse, and nothing else,' and so I thought when I writ it, and can yet conceive no other way of their operation. But I am since convinced, by the judicious Mr. Newton's incomparable book, that it is too bold a presumption to limit God's power in this point by my narrow conceptions. The gravitation of matter towards matter, by way unconceivable to me, is not only a demonstration that God can, if He pleases, put into bodies powers and ways of operation above what can be derived from our idea of body, or can be explained by what we know of matter, but also an unquestionable and everywhere visible instance that He has done so. And therefore, in the next edition of my book, I will take care to have that passage rectified. . . .

"As to self-consciousness, your lordship asks, 'What is there like self-consciousness in matter?' Nothing at all in matter as matter. But that God cannot bestow on some parcels of matter a power of thinking, and with it self-consciousness, will never be proved by asking how is it possible to apprehend that mere body should perceive that it doth perceive? The weakness of our apprehension I grant in the case: I confess as much as you please, that we cannot conceive how an unsolid created substance thinks; but this weakness of our apprehension reaches not the power of God, whose weakness is stronger than anything in man."

Lastly, Locke turns upon his opponent the power of the *odium theologicum*.

"Let it be as hard a matter as it will to give an account what it is that should keep the parts of a material soul together after it is separated from the body, yet it will be always as easy to give an account of it as to give an account what it is that shall keep together a material and immaterial substance. And yet the difficulty that there is to give an account of that, I hope, does not, with your lordship, weaken the credibility of the inseparable union of soul and body to eternity; and I persuade myself that the men of sense, to whom your lordship appeals in this case, do not find their belief of this fundamental point much weakened by that difficulty. . . . But you will say, you speak only of the soul; and your words are, that it is no easy matter to give an account how the soul should be capable of immortality unless it be a material substance. I grant it, but crave leave to say, that there is not any one of these difficulties that are or can be raised about the manner how a material soul can be immortal, which do not as well reach the immortality of the body. . . .

"But your lordship, as I guess from your following words, would argue that a material substance cannot be a free agent; whereby I suppose you only mean that you cannot see or conceive how a solid substance should begin, stop, or change its own motion. To which give me leave to answer, that when you can make it conceivable how any created, finite, dependent substance can move itself, I suppose you will find it no harder for God to bestow this power on a solid than an unsolid created substance. . . . But though you cannot see how any created substance, solid or not solid, can be a free agent (pardon me, my lord, if I put in both, till your lordship please to explain it of either, and show the manner how either of them can of itself move itself or anything else), yet I do not think you will so far deny men to be free agents, from the difficulty there is to see how they are free agents, as to doubt whether there be foundation enough for the day of judgment."

Let us now, for the sake of contrast, turn to some passages which occur in the other train of reasoning.

"If we suppose only matter and motion first or eternal, thought can never begin to be. For it is impossible to conceive that matter, either with or without motion, could have originally in and from itself sense, perception, and knowledge; as is evident from hence, that then sense, perception, and knowledge must be a property eternally inseparable from matter and every particle of it." There is a double fallacy here. In the first place, conceivability is made the unconditional test of possibility; and, in the next place, it is asserted that unless every particle of matter can think, no collocation of such particles can possibly do so. This latter fallacy is further insisted upon thus:—"If they will not allow matter as matter, that is, every particle of matter, to be as well cogitative as extended, they will have as hard a task to make out to their own reasons a cogitative being out of incogitative particles, as an extended being out of unextended parts, if I may so speak. . . . Every particle of matter, as matter, is capable of all the same figures and motions of any other; and I challenge any one in his thoughts to add anything else to one above another." Now, as we have seen, Locke himself has shown in his other trains of argument that this challenge is thoroughly futile as a refutation of possibilities; but the point to which I now wish to draw attention is this—It does not follow because certain and highly complex collocations of material particles may be supposed capable of thinking, that therefore every particle of matter must be regarded as having this attribute. We have innumerable analogies in nature of a certain collocation of matter and force producing certain results which another somewhat similar collocation could not produce: in such cases we do not assume that all the resulting attributes of the one collocation must be presented also by the other—still less that these resulting attributes must belong to the primary qualities of matter and force. Hence it is not fair to assume that thought must either be inherent in every particle of matter, or else not producible by any possible collocation of such particles, unless it has previously been shown that so to produce it by any possible collocation is in the nature of things impossible. But no one could refute this fallacy better than Locke himself has done in some of the passages already quoted from his other train of reasoning.

But to continue the quotation:—" If, therefore, it be evident that something necessarily must exist from eternity, it is also as evident that that something must necessarily be a cogitative being; for it is as impossible [*inconceivable*] that incogitative matter should produce a cogitative being, as that nothing, or the negation of all being, should produce a positive being or matter." Again, —"For unthinking particles of matter, however put together, can have [*can be taught to have*] nothing thereby added to them, but a new relation of position, which it is impossible [*inconceivable*] should give thought and knowledge to them."

It is unnecessary to multiply these quotations, for, in effect, they would all be merely repetitions of one another. It is enough to have seen that this able author undertakes to demonstrate the existence of a God, and that his whole demonstration resolves itself into the unwarrantable inference, that as we are unable to conceive how thought can be a property of matter, therefore a property of matter thought cannot be. That such an erroneous inference should occur in any writings of so old a date as those of Locke is not in itself surprising. What is surprising is the fact, that in the same writings, and in the course of the same discussion, the fallacy of this very inference is repeatedly pointed out and insisted upon in a great variety of ways; and it has been chiefly for the sake of showing the pernicious influence which preformed opinion may exert—viz., even to blinding the eyes of one of the most clear-sighted and thoughtful men that ever lived to a glaring contradiction repeated over and over again in the course of a few pages, —it has been chiefly for this reason that I have extended this Appendix to so great a length. I shall now conclude it by quoting some sentences which occur on the very next page after that from which the last quoted sentences were taken. Our author here again returns to his defence of the omnipotency of God; and as he now again thus personifies the sum total of possibility, his mind abruptly reverts to all its other class of associations. In this case the transition is particularly interesting, not only on account of its suddenness, but also because the correlations contemplated happen to be exactly the same in the two cases —viz., matter as the cause of mind, and mind as the cause of matter. Remember that on the last page this great philosopher supposed he had demonstrated the abstract impossibility of matter being the cause of mind on the ground of a causal connection being inconceivable, let us now observe what he says upon this page regarding the abstract possibility of mind being the cause of matter. "Nay, possibly, if we would emancipate ourselves from vulgar notions, and raise our thoughts as far as they would reach to a closer contemplation of things, we might be able to aim at some dim and seeming conception how matter might at first be made and begin to exist by the power of that eternal first being. . . . But you will say, Is it not impossible to admit of the making anything out of nothing, since we cannot possibly conceive it? I answer—No; because it is not reasonable to deny the power of an infinite being [this phrase, in the absence of hypothesis, *i.e.*, in Locke's other train of reasoning, is of course equivalent to the sum-total of possibility] because we cannot comprehend its operations. We do not deny other effects upon this ground, because we cannot possibly conceive the manner of their production. We cannot conceive how anything but impulse of body can move body; and yet that is not a reason sufficient to make us deny it possible, against the constant experience we have of it in ourselves, in all our voluntary motions, which are produced in us only by the free action or thought of our minds, and are not, nor can be, the effects of the impulse or determination of the blind matter in or upon our own bodies; for then it could not be in our power or choice to alter it. For example, my right hand writes, whilst my left hand is still: what causes rest in one and motion in the other? Nothing but my will, a thought in my mind; my thought only changing, the right hand rests, and the left hands moves. This is matter of fact, which cannot be denied: explain this and make it intelligible, and then the next step will be to understand creation."[1]

---

[1] All the quotations in this Appendix have been taken from the chapter on "Our knowledge of the existence of a God," and from the early part of that on "The extent of human knowledge," together with the appended letter to the Bishop of Worcester.

SUPPLEMENTARY ESSAYS.

I.

COSMIC THEISM.[1]

Mr. Herbert Spencer's doctrine of the Unknowable is a doctrine of so much speculative importance, that it behoves all students of philosophy to have clear views respecting its character and implications. Mr. Spencer has himself so fully explained the character of this doctrine, that no attentive reader can fail to understand it; but concerning those of its implications which may be termed theological —as distinguished from religious—Mr. Spencer is silent. Within the last two or three years, however, there has appeared a valuable work by an able exponent of the new philosophy; and in this work the writer, adopting his master's teaching of the Unknowable, proceeds to develop it into a definite system of what may be termed scientific theology. And not only so, but he assures the world that this system of scientific theology is the highest, the purest, and the most ennobling form of religion that mankind has ever been privileged to know in the past, or, from the nature of the case, can ever be destined to know in the future. It is a system, we are told, wherein the most fundamental truths of Theism are taught as necessary deductions from the highest truths of Science; it is a system wherein no single doctrine appeals for its acceptance to any

[1] A criticism of Mr. John Fiske's proposed system of theology as expounded in his work on "Cosmic Philosophy" (Macmillan & Co., 1874).

principle of blind or credulous faith, but wherein every doctrine can be fully justified by the searching light of reason; it is a system wherein the noblest of our aspirations and the most sublime of our emotions are able to find an object far more worthy and much more glorious than has ever been supplied to them by any of the older forms of Theism; and it is a system, therefore, in which, with a greatly enlarged and intensified meaning, we may worship God, and all that is within us bless His holy name. Assuredly a proclamation such as this, emanating from the most authoritative expounders of modern thought, as the highest and the greatest result to which a rigorous philosophic synthesis has led, is a proclamation which cannot fail to arrest our most serious attention. Nay, may it not do more than this? May it not appeal to hearts which long have ceased to worship? May it not once more revive a hope—long banished, perhaps, but still the dearest which our poor natures have experienced—that somewhere, sometime, or in some way, it may yet be possible to feel that God is not far from any one of us? For to those who have known the anguish of a shattered faith, it will not seem so childish that our hearts should beat the quicker when we once more hear a voice announcing to a world of superstitious idolaters — "Whom ye ignorantly worship, Him declare I unto you." But if, when we have listened to the glad tidings of the new gospel, we find that the preacher, though apparently in earnest, is not worthy to be heard again on this matter; and if, as we turn away, our eyes grow dim with the memory of a vanished dream, surely we may feel that the preacher is deserving of our blame for obtruding thus upon the most sacred of our sorrows.

Mr. John Fiske is, as is well known, an author who unites in himself the qualities of a well-read student of philosophy, a clear and accurate thinker, a thorough master of the principles which in his recent work he undertakes to explain and to extend, and a writer gifted in a remarkable degree with the power of lucid exposition. Such being the intellectual calibre of the man who elaborates this new system of scientific theology, I confess that, on first seeing his work, I experienced a faint hope that, in the higher departments of the Philosophy of Evolution as conceived by Mr. Spencer and elaborated by his disciple, there might be found some rational justification for an attenuated form of Theism. But on examination I find that the bread which these fathers have offered us turns out to be a stone; and thinking that it is desirable to warn other of the children — whether of the family Philosophical or Theological—against swallowing on trust a morsel so injurious, I shall endeavour to point out what I conceive to be the true nature of " Cosmic Theism."

Starting from the doctrine of the Relativity of Knowledge, Mr. Fiske, following Mr. Spencer, proceeds to show how the doctrine implies that there must be a mode of Being to which human knowledge is non-relative. Or, in other words, he shows that the postulation of phenomena necessitates the further postulation of noumena of which phenomena are the manifestations. Now what may we affirm of noumena without departing from a scientific or objective mode of philosophising? We may affirm at least this much of noumena, that they constitute a mode of existence which need not necessarily vanish were our consciousness to perish; and, therefore, that they now stand out of necessary relation to our consciousness. Or, in other words, so far as human consciousness is concerned, noumena must be regarded as absolute. "But now, what do we mean by this affirmation of absolute reality independent of the conditions of the process of knowing? Do we mean to . . . affirm, in language savouring strongly of scholasticism, that beneath the phenomena which we call subjective there is an occult substratum Mind, and beneath the phenomena which we call objective there is an occult substratum Matter? Our conclusion cannot be stated in any such form. . . . Our conclusion is simply this, that no theory of phenomena, external or internal, can be framed without postulating an Absolute Existence of which phenomena are the manifestations. And now let us carefully note what follows. We cannot identify this Absolute Existence with Mind, since what we know as Mind is a series of phenomenal manifestations. . . . Nor can we identify this Absolute Existence with Matter, since what we know as Matter is a series of phenomenal manifestations. . . . Absolute Existence, therefore,—the Reality which persists independently of us, and of which Mind and Matter are the phenomenal manifestations,—cannot be identified either with Mind or with Matter. Thus is Materialism included in the same condemnation with Idealism. . . . See then how far we have travelled from the scholastic theory of occult substrata underlying each group of phenomena. These substrata were but the ghosts of the phenomena themselves; behind the tree or the mountain a sort of phantom tree or mountain, which persists after the body of perception has gone away with the departure of the percipient mind. Clearly this is no scientific interpretation of the facts, but is rather a specimen of naïve barbaric thought surviving in metaphysics. The tree or mountain being groups of phenomena, what we assert as persisting independently of the percipient mind is a something which we are unable to condition either as tree or as mountain.

"And now we come down to the very bottom of the problem. Since we do postulate Absolute Existence, and do not postulate a particular occult substance underlying each group of phenomena, are we to be understood as implying that there is a single Being of which all phenomena, internal and external to consciousness, are manifestations? Such must seem to be the inevitable conclusion, since we are able to carry on thinking at all only under the relations of Difference and No-difference. . . . It may seem that, since we cannot attribute to the Absolute Reality any relations of Difference, we must positively ascribe to it No-difference. Or, what is the same thing, in refusing to predicate multiplicity of it, do we not virtually predicate of it unity? We do, simply because we cannot think without so doing."[1]

A single Absolute Reality being thus posited, our author proceeds, towards the close of his work, to argue that as this Reality cannot be conceived as limited either in space or time, it constitutes a Being which corresponds with our essential conception of Deity. True it is devoid of certain accessory attributes, such as personality, intelligence, and volition; but for this very reason, it is insisted, the theistic ideal as thus presented is a purer, and therefore a better, ideal than has ever been presented before. Nay, it is the highest possible form of this ideal, as the following considerations will show. In what has consisted that continuous purification of Theism which the history of thought shows to have been effected, from the grossest form of belief in supernatural agency as exhibited in Fetichism, through its more refined form as exhibited in Polytheism, to its still more refined form as exhibited in Monotheism? In nothing but in a continuous process of what Mr. Fiske calls "deanthropomorphisation." Consequently, must we not conclude that when we carry this process yet one step further, and divest our conception of Deity of all the yet lingering remnants of anthropomorphism which occur in the current conceptions of Deity, we are but still further purifying that conception? Assuredly, the attributes of personality, intelligence, and so forth, are only known as attributes of Humanity, and therefore to ascribe them to Deity is but to foster, in a more refined form, the anthropomorphic teachings of previous religions. But if we carefully refuse to limit Deity by the ascription of any human attributes whatever, and if the only attributes which we do ascribe are such as on grounds of pure reason alone we are compelled to ascribe, must we not conclude that the form of Theism which results is the purest and the most refined form in which it is possible for Theism to

[1] Cosmic Philosophy, vol. i. pp. 87–89.

exist? "From the anthropomorphic point of view it will quite naturally be urged in objection, that this apparently desirable result is reached through the degradation of Deity from an 'intelligent personality' to a 'blind force,' and is therefore in reality an undesirable and perhaps quasi-atheistic result."[1] But the question which really presents itself is, "theologically phrased, whether the creature is to be taken as a measure of the Creator. Scientifically phrased, the question is whether the highest form of Being as yet suggested to one petty race of creatures by its ephemeral experience of what is going on in one tiny corner of the universe, is necessarily to be taken as the equivalent of that absolutely highest form of Being in which all the possibilities of existence are alike comprehended."[2] Therefore, in conclusion, "whether or not it is true that, within the bounds of the phenomenal universe the highest type of existence is that which we know as humanity, the conclusion is in every way forced upon us that, quite independently of limiting conditions in space or time, there is a form of Being which can neither be assimilated to humanity nor to any lower type of existence. We have no alternative, therefore, but to regard it as higher than humanity, even 'as the heavens are higher than the earth,' and except for the intellectual arrogance which the arguments of theologians show lurking beneath their expressions of humility, there is no reason why this admission should not be made unreservedly, without the anthropomorphic qualifications by which its effect is commonly nullified. The time is surely coming when the slowness of men in accepting such a conclusion will be marvelled at, and when the very inadequacy of human language to express Divinity will be regarded as a reason for a deeper faith and more solemn adoration."[3]

I have now sufficiently detailed the leading principles of Cosmic Theism to render a clear and just conception of those fundamental parts of the system which I am about

---

[1] Cosmic Philosophy, vol. ii. pp. 429, 430.
[2] Ibid., p. 441.   [3] Ibid., pp. 450, 451.

to criticise; but it is needless to say that, for all minor details of this system, I must refer those who may not already have perused them to Mr. Fiske's somewhat elaborate essays. In now beginning my criticisms, it may be well to state at the outset, that they are to be restricted to the philosophical aspect of the subject. With matters of sentiment I do not intend to deal,—partly because to do so would be unduly to extend this essay, and partly also because I believe that, so far as the acceptance or the rejection of Cosmic Theism is to be determined by sentiment, much, if not all, will depend on individual habits of thought. For whether or not Cosmic Theism is to be regarded as a religion adapted to the needs of any individual man, will depend on what these needs are felt to be by that man himself: we cannot assert magisterially that this religion must be adapted to his needs because we have found it to be adapted to our own. And if it is retorted that, human nature being everywhere the same, a form of religion that is adapted to one man must on this account be adapted to another, I reply that it is not so. For if a man who is what Mr. Fiske calls an "Anthropomorphic Theist" finds from experience that his system of religion—say Christianity—creates and sustains a class of emotions and general habits of thought which he feels to be the highest and the best of which he is capable, it is useless for a "Cosmic Theist" to offer such a man another system of religion, in which the conditions essential to the existence of these particular emotions and habits of thought are manifestly absent. For such a man cannot but feel that the proffered substitution would be tantamount, if accepted, to an utter destruction of all that he regards as essentially religious. He will tell us that he finds it perfectly easy to understand and to appreciate those feelings of vague awe and "worship of the silent kind" which the Cosmic Theist declares to be fostered by Cosmic Theism; but he will also tell us that those feelings, which he has experienced with equal vividness under his own system of Anthropomorphic Theism, are to him but as non-religious dross compared with the unspeakable felicity of holding definite commune with the Almighty and Most Merciful, or of rendering worship that is a glad hosanna—a fearless shout of joy. On the other hand, I believe that it is possible for philosophic habits of thought so to discipline the mind that the feelings of vague awe and silent worship in the presence of an appalling Mystery become more deep and steady than a theist proper can well believe. It is therefore impossible that either party can fully appreciate those sentiments of the other which they have never fully experienced themselves; for even in those cases where an anthropomorphic theist has been compelled to abandon his creed, as the change must take place in mature life, his tone of mind has been determined before it does take place; and therefore in sentiment, though not in faith, he is more or less of a theist for the rest of his life: the only effect of the change is to create a troubled interference between his desires and his beliefs.

However, I do not intend to develop this branch of the subject further than thus to point out, in a general way, that religion-mongers as a class are apt to show too little regard for the sentiments, as distinguished from the beliefs, of those to whom they offer their wares. But although I do not intend to constitute myself a champion of theology by pointing out the defects of Cosmic Theism in the aspect which it presents to current modes of thought, there is one such defect which I must here dwell upon, because we shall afterwards have occasion to refer to it. A theologian may very naturally make this objection to Cosmic Theism as presented by Mr. Fiske—viz., that the argument on which this philosopher throughout relies as a self-evident demonstration that the new system of Theism is a further and a final improvement on all the previous systems of Theism, is a fallacious argument. As we have already seen, this argument is, that as the progress in the purification of Theism has throughout consisted in a process of "deanthropomorphisation," therefore the terminal phase in this process, which Cosmic Theism introduces, must be still in the direction of that progress. But to this argument a theologian may not unreasonably object, that this terminal phase differs from all the previous phases in one all-important feature—viz., in effecting a *total abolition* of the anthropomorphic element. Before, therefore, it can be shown that this terminal phase is a further development of *Theism*, it must be shown that Theism still remains Theism after this hitherto characteristic element has been removed. If it is true, as Mr. Fiske very properly insists, that all the various forms of belief in God have thus far had this as a common factor, that they ascribed to God the attributes of Man; it becomes a question whether we may properly abstract this hitherto invariable factor of a belief, and still call that belief by the same name. Or, to put the matter in another light, as cosmists maintain that Theism, in all the phases of its development, has been the product of a probably erroneous theory of personal agency in nature, when this theory is expressly discarded—as it is by the doctrine of the Unknowable—is it philosophically legitimate for cosmists to render their theory of things in terms which belong to the totally different theory which they discard? No doubt it is true that the progressive refinement of Theism has throughout consisted in a progressive discarding of anthropomorphic qualities; but this fact does not touch the consideration that, when we proceed to strip off the last remnants of these qualities, we are committing an act which differs *toto cœlo* from all the previous acts which are cited as precedents; for by this terminal act we are not, as heretofore, *refining* the theory of Theism—we are completely *transforming* it by removing an element which, both genetically and historically, would seem to constitute the very essence of Theism.

Or the case may be presented in yet another light. The only use of terms, whether in daily talk or in philosophical disquisition, is that of designating certain things or attributes to which by general custom we agree to affix them; so that if any one applies a term to some thing or attribute which general custom does not warrant him in so applying, he is merely laying himself open to the charge of abusing that term. Now apply these elementary principles to the case before us. We have but to think of the disgust with which the vast majority of living persons would regard the sense in which Mr. Fiske uses the term "Theism," to perceive how intimate is the association of that term with the idea of a Personal God. Such persons will feel strongly that, by this final act of purification, Mr. Fiske has simply purified the Deity altogether out of existence. And I scarcely think it is here competent to reply that all previous acts of purification were at first similarly regarded as destructive, because it is evident that none of these previous acts affected, as this one does, the central core of Theism. And, lastly, if it should be still further objected, that by declaring the theory of Personal Agency the central core of Theism, I am begging the question as to the appropriateness of Mr. Fiske's use of the word "Theism,"— seeing he appears to regard the essential meaning of this word to be that of a postulation of merely Causal Agency, —I answer, More of this anon; but meanwhile let it be observed that any charge of question-begging lies rather at the door of Mr. Fiske, in that he assumes, without any expressed justification, that the essence of Theism *does* consist in such a postulation and in nothing more. And as he unquestionably has against him the present world of theists no less than the history of Theism in the past, I do not see how he is to meet this charge except by confessing to an abuse of the term in question.

I will now proceed to examine the structure of Cosmic Theism. We are all, I suppose, at one in allowing that there are only three "verbally intelligible" theories of the universe,—viz., that it is self-existent, or that it is self-created, or that it has been created by some other and external Being. It is usual to call the first of these theories

Atheism, the second Pantheism, and the third Theism. Now as there are here three distinct nameable theories, it is necessary, if the term "Cosmic Theism" is to be justified as an appropriate term, that the particular theory which it designates should be shown to be in its essence theistic— *i.e.*, that the theory should present those distinguishing features in virtue of which Theism differs from Atheism on the one hand, and from Pantheism on the other. Now what are these features? The postulate of an Eternal Self-existing Something is common to Theism and to Atheism. Here Atheism ends. Theism, however, is generally said to assume Personality, Intelligence, and Creative Power as attributes of the single self-existing substance. Lastly, Pantheism assumes the Something now existing to have been self-created. To which, then, of these distinct theories is Cosmic Theism most nearly allied? For the purpose of answering this question, I shall render that theory in terms of a formula which Mr. Fiske presents as a full and complete statement of the theory:—"*There exists a* POWER, *to which no limit in space or time is conceivable, of which all phenomena, as presented in consciousness, are manifestations, but which we can only know through these manifestations.*" But although the word "Power" is here so strongly emphasised, we are elsewhere told that it is not to be regarded as having more than a strictly relative or symbolic meaning; so that, in point of fact, some more neutral word, such as "Something," "Being," or "Substance," ought in strictness to be here substituted for the word "Power." Well, if this is done, we have the postulation of a Being which is self-existing, infinite, and eternal—relatively, at all events, to our powers of conception. Thus far, therefore, it would seem that we are still on the common standing-ground of Atheism, Pantheism, and Theism; for as it is not, so far as I can see, incumbent on Pantheism to affirm that "thought is a measure of things," the *apparent* or *relative* eternity which the Primal Something must be supposed to present may not be *actual* or *absolute* eternity. Nevertheless, as Mr. Fiske, by predicating Divinity of the Primal Something, implicitly attributes to it the quality of an *eternal* self-existence, I infer that Cosmic Theism may be concluded at this point to part company with Pantheism. There remain, then, Theism and Atheism.

Now undoubtedly, at first sight, Cosmic Theism appears to differ from Atheism in one all-important particular. For we have seen that, by means of a subtle though perfectly logical argument, Cosmic Philosophy has evolved this conclusion—that all phenomena as presented in consciousness are manifestations of a not improbable Single Self-existing Power, of whose existence these manifestations alone can make us cognisant. From which it apparently follows, that this hypothetical Power must be regarded as existing out of necessary relation to the phenomenal universe; that it is, therefore, beyond question "Absolute Being;" and that, as such, we are entitled to call it Deity. But in the train of reasoning of which this is a very condensed epitome, it is evident that the legitimacy of denominating this Absolute Being Deity, must depend on the exact meaning which we attach to the word "Absolute"—and this, be it observed, quite apart from the question, before touched upon, as to whether Personality and Intelligence are not to be considered as attributes essential to Deity. In what sense, then, is the word "Absolute" used? It is used in this sense. As from the relativity of knowledge we cannot know things in themselves, but only symbolical representations of such things, therefore things in themselves are absolute to consciousness: but analysis shows that we cannot conceivably predicate Difference among things in themselves, so that we are at liberty, with due diffidence, to predicate of them No-difference: hence the noumena of the schoolmen admit of being collected into a *summum genus* of noumenal existence; and since, before their colligation noumena were severally absolute, after their colligation they become collectively absolute: therefore it is legitimate to designate this sum-total of noumenal existence, "Absolute Being." Now there is clearly no exception to be taken to the formal accuracy of this reasoning; the only question is as to whether the "Absolute Being" which it evolves is absolute in the sense required by Theism. I confess that to me this Being appears to be absolute in a widely different sense from that in which Deity must be regarded as absolute. For this Being is thus seen to be absolute in no other sense than as holding —to quote from Mr. Fiske—"existence independent of the conditions of the process of knowing." In other words, it is absolute only as standing out of necessary relation to *human consciousness*. But Theism requires, as an essential feature, that Deity should be absolute as standing out of necessary relation to *all else*. Before, therefore, the Absolute Being of Cosmism can be shown, by the reasoning adopted, to deserve, even in part, the appellation of Deity, it must be shown that there is no other mode of Being in existence save our own subjective consciousness and the Absolute Reality which becomes objective to it through the world of phenomena. But any attempt to establish this position would involve a disregard of the doctrine that knowledge is relative; and to do this, it is needless to say, would be to destroy the basis of the argument whereby the Absolute Being of Cosmism was posited.

Or, to state this part of the criticism in other words, as the first step in justifying the predication of Deity, it must be shown that the Being of which the predication is made is absolute, and this not merely as independent of human consciousness, but as independent of the whole noumenal universe—Deity itself alone excepted. That is, the Being of which Deity is predicated must be Unconditioned. Hence it is incumbent on Cosmic Theism to prove, either that the Causal Agent which it denominates Deity is itself the whole noumenal universe, or that it created the rest of a noumenal universe; else there is nothing to show that this Causal Agent was not itself created—seeing that, even if we assume the existence of a God, there is nothing to indicate that the Causal Agent of Cosmism is that God.

It would appear therefore from this, that whatever else the Cosmist's theory of things may be, it certainly is not Theism; and I think that closer inspection will tend to confirm this judgment. To this then let us proceed.

Mr. Fiske is very hard on the atheists, and so will probably repudiate with scorn any insinuations to the effect that his theory of things is "quasi-atheistic." Nevertheless, it seems to me that he is very unjust to the atheists, in that while he spares no pains to "purify" and "refine" the theory of the theists, so as at last to leave nothing but what he regards as the distilled essence of Theism behind; he habitually leaves the theory of the atheists as he finds it, without making any attempt either to "purify" it by removing its weak and unnecessary ingredients, or to "refine" it by adding such sublimated ingredients as modern speculation has supplied. Thus, while he despises the atheists of the eighteenth century for their irrationality in believing in the self-existence of a *phenomenal* universe, and reviles them for their irreligion in denying that "the religious sentiment needed satisfaction;" he does not wait to inquire whether, in its essential substance, the theory of these men is not the one that has proved itself best able to withstand the grinding action of more recent thought. But let us in fairness ask, What was the essential substance of that theory? Apparently it was the bare statement of the unthinkable fact that Something Is. It therefore seems to me useless in Mr. Fiske to lay so much stress on the fact that this Something was originally identified by atheists with the phenomenal universe. It seems useless to do this, because such identification is clearly no part of the *essence* of Atheism, which, as just stated, I take to consist in the single dogma of self-existence as itself sufficient to constitute a theory of things. And, if so, it is a matter of scarcely any moment, as regards that theory, whether we are *immediately* cognisant of that which is self-existent, or only become so through the world of phenomena—the vital point of the theory being, that Self-existence, *wherever posited*, is itself the only admissible explanation of phenomena. Or, in other words, it does not seem that there is anything in the atheistic theory, as such, which is incompatible with the doctrine of the Relativity of Knowledge; so that whatever cogency there may be in the train of reasoning whereby a single Causal Agent is deduced from that doctrine, it would seem that an atheist has as much right to the benefit of this reasoning as a theist; and there is thus no more apparent reason why this single Causal Agent should be appropriated as the God of Theism, than that it should be appropriated as the Self-existing X of Atheism. Indeed, there seems to be less reason. For an atheist of to-day may very properly argue :—' So far from beholding anything divine in this Single Being absolute to human consciousness, it is just precisely the form of Being which my theory postulates as the Self-existing All. In order to constitute such a Being God, it must be shown, as we have already seen, to be something more than a merely Causal Agent which is absolute in the grotesquely restricted sense of being independent of 'one petty race of creatures with an ephemeral experience of what is going on in one tiny corner of the universe;' it must be shown to be something more than absolute even in the wholly unrestricted sense of being Unconditioned; it must be shown to possess such other attributes as are distinctive of Deity. For I maintain that even Unconditioned Being, *merely as such*, would only then have a right to the name of God when it has been shown that the theory of Theism has a right to monopolise the doctrine of Relativity.'

In thus endeavouring to " purify " the theory of Atheism,

by divesting it of all superfluous accessories, and laying bare what I conceive to be its essential substance; it may be well to state that, even apart from their irreligious character, I have no sympathy with the atheists of the past century. I mean, that these men do not seem to me to deserve any credit for advanced powers of speculation merely because they adopted a theory of things which in its essential features now promises to be the most enduring. For it is evident that the strength of this theory now lies in its *simplicity*,—in its undertaking to explain, so far as explanation is possible, the sum-total of phenomena by the single postulate of self-existence. But it seems to me that in the last century there were no sufficient data for rendering such a theory of things a rational theory; for so long as the quality of self-existence was supposed to reside in phenomena themselves, the very simplicity of the theory, as expressed in words, must have seemed to render it inapplicable as a reasonable theory of things. The astounding variety, complexity, and harmony which are everywhere so conspicuous in the world of phenomena must have seemed to necessitate as an explanation some one integrating cause; and it is impossible that in the eighteenth century any such integrating cause can have been conceivable other than Intelligence. Therefore I think, with Mr. Fiske, that the atheists of the eighteenth century were irrational in applying their single postulate of self-existence as alone a sufficient explanation of things. But of course the aspect of the case is now completely changed, when we regard it in all the flood of light which has been shed on it by recent science, physical and speculative. For the demonstration of the fact that energy is indestructible, coupled with the corollary that every so-called natural law is a physically necessary consequence of that fact, clearly supply us with a completely novel datum as the ultimate source of experience—and a datum, moreover, which is as different as can well be imagined from the ever-changing, ever-fleeting, world of phenomena. We have, therefore, but to apply the postulate of self-existence to this single ultimate datum, and we have a theory of things as rational as the Atheism of the last century was irrational. Nevertheless, that this theory is more akin to the Atheism of the last century than to any other theory of that time, is, I think, unquestionable; for while we retain the central doctrine of self-existence as alone a scientifically admissible, or non-gratuitous, explanation of things, we only change the original theory by transferring the application of this doctrine from the world of manifestations to that which causes the manifestations: we do not resort to any of the *additional* doctrines whereby the other theories of the universe were distinguished from the theory of Atheism in its original form. However, as by our recognition of the relativity of knowledge we are precluded from dogmatically denying any theory of the universe that may be proposed, it would clearly be erroneous to identify the doctrine of the Unknowable with the theory of Atheism: all we can say is, that, so far as speculative thought can soar, the permanent self-existence of an inconceivable Something, which manifests itself to consciousness as force and matter, constitutes the only datum that can be shown to be required for the purposes of a rational ontology.

To sum up. In the theory which Mr. Fiske calls Cosmic Theism, while I am able to discern the elements which I think may properly be regarded as common to Theism and to Atheism, I am not able to discern any single element that is specifically distinctive of Theism. Still I am far from concluding that the theory in question is the theory of Atheism. All I wish to insist upon is this—that as the Absolute Being of Cosmism presents no other qualities than such as are required by the renovated theory of Atheism, its postulation supplies a basis, not for Theism, but for Non-theism: a man with such a postulate ought in strictness to abstain from either affirming or denying the existence of God. And this, I may observe, appears to be the position which Mr. Spencer himself has adopted as the only logical outcome of his doctrine of the Unknowable—a position which, in my opinion, it is most undesirable to obscure by endeavouring to give it a quasi-theistic interpretation. I may further observe, that we here seem to have a philosophical justification of the theological sentiment previously alluded to—the sentiment, namely, that by his attempt at a final purification of Theism, Mr. Fiske has destroyed those essential features of the theory in virtue of which alone it exists as Theism. For seeing it is impossible, from the relativity of knowledge, that the Absolute Being of Cosmism can ever be shown absolute in the sense required by Theism, and, even if it could, that it would still be but the Unconditioned Being of Atheism; it follows that if this Absolute Being is to be shown even in part to deserve the appellation of Deity, it must be shown to possess the only remaining attributes which are distinctive of Deity—to wit, personality and intelligence. But forasmuch as the final act of purifying the conception of Deity consists, according to Mr. Fiske, in expressly removing these particular attributes from the object of that conception, does it not follow that the conception which remains is, as I have said, not theistic, but non-theistic?

Here my criticism might properly have ended, were it not that Mr. Fiske, after having divested the Deity of all his psychical attributes, forthwith proceeds to show how it may be dimly possible to reinvest him with attributes that are "quasi-psychical." Mr. Fiske is, of course, far too subtle a thinker not to see that his previous argument from relativity precludes him from assigning much weight to the ontological speculations in which he here indulges, seeing that in whatever degree the relativity of knowledge renders legitimate the non-ascription to Deity of known psychical attributes, in some such degree at least must it render illegitimate the ascription to Deity of unknown psychical attributes. But in the part of his work in which he treats of the quasi-psychical attributes, Mr. Fiske is merely engaged in showing that the speculative standing of the "materialists" is inferior to that of the "spiritualists;" so that, as this is a subject distinct from Theism, he is not open to the charge of inconsistency. Well, feeble as these speculations undoubtedly are in the support which they render to Theism, it nevertheless seems desirable to consider them before closing this review. The speculations in question are quoted from Mr. Spencer, and are as follows:—

"Mind, as known to the possessor of it, is a circumscribed aggregate of activities; and the cohesion of these activities, one with another, throughout the aggregate, compels the postulation of a something of which they are the activities. But the same experiences which make him aware of this coherent aggregate of mental activities, simultaneously make him aware of activities that are not included in it—outlying activities which become known by their effects on this aggregate, but which are experimentally proved to be not coherent with it, and to be coherent with one another (*First Principles*, §§ 43, 44). As, by the definition of them, these external activities cannot be brought within the aggregate of activities distinguished as those of Mind, they must for ever remain to him nothing more than the unknown correlatives of their effects on this aggregate; and can be thought of only in terms furnished by this aggregate. Hence, if he regards his conceptions of these activities lying beyond Mind as constituting knowledge of them, he is deluding himself: he is but representing these activities in terms of Mind, and can never do otherwise. Eventually he is obliged to admit that his ideas of Matter and Motion, merely symbolic of unknowable realities, are complex states of consciousness built out of units of feeling. But if, after admitting this, he persists in asking whether units of feeling are of the same nature as the units of force distinguished as external, or whether the units of force distinguished as external are of the same nature as units of feeling; then the reply, still substantially the same, is that we may go further towards conceiving units of external force to be identical with units of feeling, than we can towards conceiving units of feeling to be identical with units of external force. Clearly, if units of external force are regarded as absolutely unknown and unknowable, then to translate units of feeling into them is to translate the known into the unknown, which is absurd. And if they are what they are supposed to be by those who identify them with their symbols, then the difficulty of translating units of feeling into them is insurmountable: if Force as it objectively exists is absolutely alien in nature from that which exists subjectively as Feeling, then the transformation of Force into Feeling is unthinkable. Either way, therefore, it is impossible to interpret inner existence in terms of outer existence. But if, on the other hand, units of Force as they exist objectively are essentially the same in nature with those manifested subjectively as units of Feeling, then a conceivable hypothesis remains open. Every element of that aggregate of activities constituting a consciousness is known as belonging to consciousness only by its cohesion with the rest. Beyond the limits of this coherent aggregate of activities exist activities quite independent of it, and which cannot be brought into it. We may imagine, then, that by their exclusion from the circumscribed activities constituting consciousness, these outer activities, though of the same intrinsic nature, become antithetically opposed in aspect. Being disconnected from consciousness, or cut off by its limits, they are thereby rendered foreign to it. Not being incorporated with its activities, or linked with these as they are with one another, consciousness cannot, as it were, run through them; and so they come to be figured as unconscious—are symbolised as having the nature called material, as opposed to that called spiritual. While, however, it thus seems an imaginable possibility that units of external Force may be identical in nature with units of the force known as Feeling, yet we cannot by so representing them get any nearer to a comprehension of external Force. For, as already shown, supposing all forms of Mind to be composed of homogeneous units of feeling variously aggregated, the resolution of them into such units leaves us as unable as before to think of the substance of Mind as it exists in such units; and thus, even could we really figure to ourselves all units of external Force as being essentially like units of the force known as Feeling, and as so constituting a universal sentiency, we should be as far as ever from forming a conception of that which is universally sentient." [1]

Now while I agree with Mr. Fiske that we have here "the most subtle conclusion now within the ken of the scientific speculator, reached without any disregard of the canons prescribed by the doctrine of relativity," I would like to point out to minds less clear-sighted than his, that this same "doctrine of relativity" effectually debars us from using this "conclusion" as an argument of any assignable value in favour of Theism. For the value of conceivability as a test of truth, on which this conclusion is founded, is here vitiated by the consideration that, *whatever* the nature of Force-units may be, we can clearly perceive it to be a subjective necessity of the case that they should admit of being more easily conceived by us to be of the nature of Feeling-units than to be of any other nature. For as units of Feeling are the only entities of which we are, or can be, conscious, they are the entities into which units of Force must be, so to speak, subjectively translated before we can cognise their existence at all. Therefore, *whatever* the real nature of Force-units may be, ultimate analysis must show that it is more conceivable to identify them in thought with the only units of which we are cognisant, than it is to think of them as units of which we are not cognisant, and concerning which, therefore, conception is necessarily impossible. Or thus, the only

[1] **Principles of Psychology, vol. i. pp. 159–161.**

alternative with respect to the classifying of Force-units lies between refusing to classify them at all, or classifying them with the only ultimate units with which we are acquainted. But this restriction, for aught that can ever be shown to the contrary, arises only from the subjective conditions of our own consciousness; there is nothing to indicate that, in objective reality, units of Force are in any wise akin to units of Feeling. Conceivability, therefore, as a test of truth, is in this particular case of no assignable degree of value; for as the entities to which it is applied are respectively the highest known abstractions of subjective and objective existence, the test of conceivability is neutralised by directly encountering the inconceivable relation that subsists between subject and object. I think, therefore, it is evident that these ontological speculations present no sufficient warrant for an inference, even of the slenderest kind, that the Absolute Being of Cosmism possesses attributes of a nature quasi-psychical; and, if so, it follows that these speculations are incompetent to form the basis of a theory which, even by the greatest stretch of courtesy, can in any legitimate sense be termed quasi-theistic.[1]

[1] We thus see that the question whether there may not be "something quasi-psychical in the constitution of things" is a question which does not affect the position of Theism as it has been left by a negation of the self-conscious personality of God. But as the speculations on which this question has been reared are in themselves of much philosophical interest, I may here observe that, in one form or another, they have been dimly floating in men's minds for a long time past. Thus, excepting the degree of certainty with which it is taught, we have in Mr. Spencer's words above quoted a reversion to the doctrine of Buddha; for, as "force is persistent," all that would happen on death, supposing the doctrine true, would be an escape of the "circumscribed aggregate" of units forming the individual consciousness into the unlimited abyss of similar units constituting the "Absolute Being" of the Cosmists, or the "Divine Essence" of the Buddhists. Again, the doctrine in a vague form pervades the philosophy of Spinoza, and is next clearly enunciated by Wundt. Lastly, in a recently published very remarkable essay "On the Nature of Things in Themselves," Professor Clifford arrives at a similar doctrine by a different route. The following is the conclusion to which he arrives:—"That element of which, as we have seen, even the simplest feeling is a complex, I shall call *Mind-stuff*. A moving molecule of inorganic matter does not possess mind or conscious-

On the whole, then, I conclude that the term "Cosmic Theism" is not an appropriate term whereby to denote the theory of things set forth in "Cosmic Philosophy;" and that it would therefore be more judicious to leave the doctrine of the Unknowable as Mr. Spencer has left it— that is, without theological implications of any kind. But in now taking leave of this subject, I should like it to be understood that the only reason why I have ventured thus to take exception to a part of Mr. Fiske's work is because I regret that a treatise which displays so much of literary excellence and philosophic power should lend itself to promoting what I regard as mistaken views concerning the ontological tendencies of recent thought, and this with no other apparent motive than that of unworthily retaining in the new philosophy a religious term the distinctive connotations of which are considered by that philosophy to have become obsolete.

ness, but it possesses a small piece of mind-stuff. When molecules are so combined together as to form the film on the under side of a jellyfish, the elements of mind-stuff which go along with them are so combined as to form the faint beginnings of Sentience. When the molecules are so combined as to form the brain and nervous system of a vertebrate, the corresponding elements of mind-stuff are so combined as to form some kind of consciousness; that is to say, changes in the complex which take place at the same time get so linked together that the repetition of one implies the repetition of the other. When matters take the complex form of a living human brain, the corresponding mind-stuff takes the form of a human consciousness, having intelligence and volition." (Mind, January, 1878.)

II.

SUPPLEMENTARY ESSAY IN REPLY TO A RECENT WORK ON THEISM.[1]

On perusing my main essay several years after its completion, it occurred to me that another very effectual way of demonstrating the immense difference between the nature of all previous attacks upon the teleological argument and the nature of the present attack, would be briefly to review the reasonable objections to which all the previous attacks were open. Very opportunely a work on Theism has just been published which states these objections with great lucidity, and answers them with much ability. The work to which I allude is by the Rev. Professor Flint, and as it is characterised by temperate candour in tone and logical care in exposition, I felt on reading it that the work was particularly well suited for displaying the enormous change in the speculative standing of Theism which the foregoing considerations must be rationally deemed to have effected. I therefore determined on throwing my supplementary essay, which I had previously intended to write, into the form of a criticism on Professor Flint's treatise, and I adopted this course the more willingly because there are several other points dwelt upon in that treatise which it seems desirable for me to consider in the present one, although, for the sake of conciseness, I abstained from discussing them in my previous essay.

[1] **Theism**, by Robert Flint, D.D., LL.D., Professor of Divinity in the University of Edinburgh, &c.

With these two objects in view, therefore, I undertook the following criticism.[1]

In the first place, it is needful to protest against an argument which our author adopts on the authority of Professor Clark Maxwell. The argument is now a well-known one, and is thus stated by Professor Maxwell in his presidential address before the British Association for the Advancement of Science, 1870:—"None of the processes of nature, since the time when nature began, have produced the slightest difference in the properties of any molecule. We are therefore unable to ascribe either the existence of the molecules or the identity of their properties to the operation of any of the causes which we call natural. On the other hand, the exact quality of each molecule to all others of the same kind gives it, as Sir John Herschel has well said, the essential character of a manufactured article, and precludes the idea of its being eternal and self-existent. Thus we have been led along a strictly scientific path, very near to the point at which science must stop. Not that science is debarred from studying the external mechanism of a molecule which she cannot take to pieces, any more than from investigating an organism which she cannot put together. But in tracing back the history of matter, science is arrested when

---

[1] Such being the objects in view, I have not thought it necessary to extend this criticism into anything resembling a review of Professor Flint's work as a whole; but, on the contrary, I have aimed rather at confining my observations to those parts of his treatise which embody the current arguments from teleology alone. I may here observe, however, in general terms, that I consider all his arguments to have been answered by anticipation in the foregoing examination of Theism. I may also here observe, that throughout the following essay I have used the word "design" in the sense in which it is used by Professor Flint himself. This sense is distinctly a different one from that which the word bears in the writings of the Paley, Bell, and Chalmers school. For while in the latter writings, as pointed out in Chapter III., the word bears its natural meaning of a certain *process of thought*, in Professor Flint's work it is used rather as expressive of a *product of intelligence*. In other words, "design," as used by Professor Flint, is synonymous with *intention*, irrespective of the particular psychological process by which the intention may have been put into effect.

she assures herself, on the one hand, that the molecule has been made, and, on the other, that it has not been made by any of the processes we call natural."

Now it is obvious that we have here no real argument, since it is obvious that science can never be in a position to assert that atoms, the very existence of which is hypothetical, were never "made by any of the processes we call natural." The mere fact that in the universe, as we now know it, the evolution of material atoms is not observed to be taking place "by any of the processes we call natural," cannot possibly be taken as proof, or even as presumption, that there ever was a time when the material atoms now in existence were created by a supernatural cause. The fact cannot be taken to justify any such inference for the following reasons. In the first place, assuming the atomic theory to be true, and there is nothing in the argument to show that the now-existing atoms are not self-existing atoms, endowed with their peculiar and severally distinctive properties from all eternity. Doubtless the argument is, that as there appear to be some sixty or more elementary atoms constituting the raw material of the observable universe, it is incredible that they can all have owed their correlated properties to any cause other than that of a designing and manufacturing intelligence. But, in the next place—and here comes the demolishing force of the criticism—science is not in a position to assert that these sixty or more elementary atoms are in any real sense of the term elementary. The mere fact that chemistry is as yet in too undeveloped a condition to pronounce whether or not all the forms of matter known to her are modifications of some smaller number of elements, or even of a single element, cannot possibly be taken as a warrant for so huge an inference as that there are really more than sixty elements all endowed with absolutely distinctive properties by a supernatural cause. Now this consideration, which arises immediately from the doctrine of the relativity of knowledge, is alone amply sufficient to destroy the present argument. But we must not on this account lose sight of the fact that, even to our strictly relative science in its present embryonic condition, we are not without decided indications, not only that the so-called elements are probably for the most part compounds, but even that matter as a whole is one substance, which is itself probably but some modification of energy. Indeed, the whole tendency of recent scientific speculation is towards the view that the universe consists of some one substance, which, whether self-existing or created, is diverse only in its relation to ignorance. And if this view is correct, how obvious is the inference which I have elaborated in § 32, that all the diverse forms of matter, as we know them, were probably evolved by natural causes. So obvious, indeed, is this inference, that to resort to any supernatural hypothesis to explain the diverse properties of the various chemical elements appears to me a most glaring violation of the law of parcimony—as much more glaring, for instance, than the violation of this law by Paley, as the number and variety of organic species are greater than the number and variety of chemical species. And if it was illegitimate in Paley to use a mere absence of knowledge as to how the transmutation of apparently fixed species of animals was effected as equivalent to the possession of knowledge that such transmutation had not been effected, how much more illegitimate must it be to commit a similar sin against logic in the case of the chemical elements, where our classification is confessedly beset with numberless difficulties, and when we begin to discern that in all probability it is a classification essentially artificial. Lastly, the mere fact that the transmutation of chemical species and the evolution of chemical "atoms" are processes which we do not now observe as occurring in nature, is surely a consideration of a far more feeble kind than it is even in the case of biological species and biological evolution; seeing that nature's laboratory must be now so inconceivably different from what it was during the condensation of the nebula. What an atrocious piece of arrogance, therefore, it is to assert that " none of the processes of nature, *since the time when nature began*, have produced the slightest difference in the properties of any molecule!" No one can entertain a higher respect for Professor Clark Maxwell than I do; but a single sentence of such a kind as this cannot leave two opinions in any impartial mind concerning his competency to deal with such subjects.

I am therefore sorry to see this absurd argument approvingly incorporated in Professor Flint's work. He says, " I believe that no reply to these words of Professor Clark Maxwell is possible from any one who holds the ordinary view of scientific men as to the ultimate constitution of matter. They must suppose every atom, every molecule, to be of such a nature, to be so related to others and to the universe generally, that things may be such as we see them to be; but this their fitness to be built up into the structure of the universe is a proof that they have been made fit, and since natural forces could not have acted on them while not yet existent, a supernatural power must have created them, and created them with a view to their manifold uses." Here the inference so confidently drawn would have been a weak one even were we not able to see that the doctrine of natural evolution probably applies to inorganic nature no less than to organic. For the inference is drawn from considerations of a character so transcendental and so remote from science, that unless we wish to be deceived by a merely verbal argument, we must feel that the possibilities of error in the inference are so numerous and indefinite, that the inference itself is well-nigh worthless as a basis of belief. But when we add that in Chapter IV. of the foregoing essay it has been shown to be within the legitimate scope of scientific reasoning to conclude that material atoms have been progressively evolved *pari passu* with the natural laws of chemical combination, it is evident that any force which the present argument could ever have had must now be pronounced as neutralised. Natural causes have been shown, so far as scientific inference can extend, as not improbably sufficient to produce the observed effects; and therefore we are no longer free to invoke the hypothetical action of any supernatural cause.

The same observations apply to Professor Flint's theistic argument drawn from recent scientific speculations as to the vortex-ring construction of matter. If these speculations are sound, their only influence on Theism would be that of supplying a scientific demonstration of the substantial identity of Force and Matter, and so of supplying a still more valid basis for the theory as to the natural genesis of matter from a single primordial substance, in the manner sketched out in Chapter IV. For the argument adduced by Professor Flint, that as the manner in which the vorticial motion of a ring is originated has not as yet been suggested, therefore its origination must have been due to a "Divine impulse," is an argument which again uses the absence of knowledge as equivalent to its possession. We are in the presence of a very novel and highly abstruse theory, or rather hypothesis, in physics, which was originally suggested by, and has hitherto been mainly indebted to, empirical experiments as distinguished from mathematical calculations; and from the mere fact that, in the case of such a hypothesis, mathematicians have not as yet been able to determine the physical conditions required to originate vorticial motion, we are expected to infer that no such conditions can ever have existed, and therefore that every such vortex system, if it exists, is a miracle!

And substantially the same criticism applies to the argument which Professor Flint adduces—the argument also on which Professors Balfour and Tait lay so much stress in their work on the *Unseen Universe*—the argument, namely, as to the non-eternal character of heat.

The calculations on which this argument depends would only be valid as sustaining this argument if they were based upon a knowledge of the universe *as a whole;* and therefore, as before, the absence of requisite knowledge must not be used as equivalent to its possession.

These, however, are the weakest parts of Professor Flint's work. I therefore gladly turn to those parts which are exceedingly cogent as written from his standpoint, but which, in view of the strictures on the teleological argument that I have adduced in Chapters IV. and VI., I submit to be now wholly valueless.

"How could matter of itself produce order, even if it were self-existent and eternal? It is far more unreasonable to believe that the atoms or constituents of matter produced of themselves, without the action of a Supreme Mind, this wonderful universe, than that the letters of the English alphabet produced the plays of Shakespeare, without the slightest assistance from the human mind known by that famous name. These atoms might, perhaps, now and then, here and there, at great distances and long intervals, produce by a chance contact some curious collocation or compound; but never could they produce order or organisation on an extensive scale, or of a durable character, unless ordered, arranged, and adjusted in ways of which intelligence alone can be the ultimate explanation. To believe that these fortuitous and indirected movements could originate the universe, and all the harmonies and utilities and beauties which abound in it, evinces a credulity far more extravagant than has ever been displayed by the most superstitious of religionists. Yet no consistent materialist can refuse to accept this colossal chance hypothesis. All the explanations of the order of the universe which materialists, from Democritus and Epicurus to Diderot and Lange, have devised, rest on the assumption that the elements of matter, being eternal, must pass through infinite combinations, and that one of these must be our present world—a special collocation among the countless millions of collocations, past and future. Throw the letters of the Greek alphabet, it has been said, an infinite number of times, and you must produce the 'Iliad' and all the Greek books. The theory of probabilities, I need hardly say, requires us to believe nothing so absurd. . . . But what is the 'Iliad' to the hymn of creation and the drama of providence?" &c.

Now this I conceive to have been a fully valid argument at the time it was published, and indeed the most convincing of all the arguments in favour of Theism. But, as already so frequently pointed out, the considerations adduced in Chapter IV. of the present work are utterly destructive of this argument. For this argument assumes, rightly enough, that the only alternative we have in choosing our hypothesis concerning the final explanation of things is either to regard that explanation as Intelligence or as Fortuity. This, I say, was a legitimate argument a few months ago, because up to that time no one had shown that strictly natural causes, as distinguished from chances, could conceivably be able to produce a cosmos; and although the several previous writers to whom Professor Flint alludes—and he might have alluded to others in this connection—entertained a dim anticipation of the fact that natural causes might alone be sufficient to produce the observed universe, still these dim anticipations were worthless as *arguments* so long as it remained impossible to suggest any natural *principle* whereby such a result could have been conceivably effected by such causes. But it is evident that Professor Flint's time-honoured argument is now completely overthrown, unless it can be proved that there is some radical error in the reasoning whereby I have endeavoured to show that natural causes not only *may*, but *must*, have produced existing order. The overthrow is complete, because the very groundwork of the argument in question is knocked away; a third possibility, of the nature of a necessity, is introduced, and therefore the alternative is no longer between Intelligence and Fortuity, but between Intelligence and Natural Causation. Whereas the overwhelming strength of the argument from Order has hitherto consisted in the supposition of Intelligence as the one and only conceivable cause of the integration of things, my exposition in Chapter IV. has shown that such integration must have been due, at all events in a relative or proximate sense, to a strictly physical cause—the persistence of force and the consequent self-evolution of natural law. And the question as to whether or not Intelligence may not have been the absolute or ultimate cause is manifestly a question altogether alien to the argument from Order; for if existing order admits of being accounted for, in a relative or proximate sense, by merely physical causes, the argument from a relative or proximate order is not at liberty to infer or to assume the existence of any higher or more ultimate cause. Although, therefore, in Chapter V., I have been careful to point out that the fact of existing order having been due to proximate or natural causes does not actually *disprove* the possible existence of an ultimate and supernatural cause, still it must be carefully observed that this *negative* fact cannot possibly justify any *positive* inference to the existence of such a cause.

Thus, upon the whole, it may be said, without danger of reasonable dispute, that as the argument from Order has hitherto derived its immense weight entirely from the fact that Intelligence appeared to be the one and only cause sufficient to produce the observed integration of the cosmos, this immense weight has now been completely counterpoised by the demonstration that other causes of a strictly physical kind must have been instrumental, if not themselves alone sufficient, to produce this integration. So that, just as in the case of Astronomy the demonstration of the one natural principle of gravity was sufficient to classify under one physical explanation several observed facts which many persons had previously attributed to supernatural causes; and just as in the more complex science of Geology the demonstration of the one principle of uniformitarianism was sufficient to explain, without the aid of supernaturalism, a still greater number of facts; and, lastly, just as in the case of the still more complex science of Biology the demonstration of the one principle of natural selection was sufficient to marshal under one scientific, or natural, hypothesis an almost incalculable number of facts which were previously explained by the metaphysical hypothesis of supernatural design; so in the science which includes all other sciences, and which we may term the science of Cosmology, I assert with confidence that in the one principle of the persistence of force we have a demonstrably harmonising principle, whereby all the facts within our experience admit of being collocated under one natural explanation, without there being the smallest reason to attribute these facts to any supernatural cause.

But perhaps the immense change which these considerations must logically be regarded as having produced in the speculative standing of the argument from teleology will be better appreciated if I continue to quote from Professor Flint's very forcible and thoroughly logical exposition of the previous standing of this argument. He says:—

"To ascribe the origination of order to *law* is a manifest evasion of the real problem. Law is order. Law is the very thing to be explained. The question is—Has law a reason, or is it without a reason? The unperverted human mind cannot believe it to be without a reason."

I do not know where a more terse and accurate statement of the case could be found; and to my mind the question so lucidly put admits of the direct answer—Law clearly has a reason of a purely physical kind. And therefore I submit that the following quotation which Professor Flint makes from Professor Jevons, logical as it was when written, must now be regarded as embodying an argument which is obsolete.

"As an unlimited number of atoms can be placed in unlimited space in an unlimited number of modes of distribution, there must, even granting matter to have had all its laws from eternity, have been at some moment in time, out of the unlimited choices and distributions possible, that one choice and distribution which yielded the fair and orderly universe that now exists. Only out of rational choice can order have come."

But clearly the alternative is now no longer one between chance and choice. If natural laws arise by way of necessary consequence from the persistence of a single self-existing substance, it becomes a matter of scientific (though not of logical) demonstration that "the fair and orderly universe that now exists" is the one and only universe that, in the nature of things, *can* exist. But to continue this interesting passage from Dr. Flint's work—interesting not only because it sets forth the previous standing of this subject with so much clearness, but also because the work is of such very recent publication.

"The most common mode, perhaps, of evading the problem which order presents to reason is the indication of the process by which the order has been realised. From Democritus to the latest Darwinian there have been men who supposed they had completely explained away the evidences of design in nature when they had described the physical antecedents of the arrangements appealed to as evidences. Aristotle showed the absurdity of this supposition more than 2200 years ago."

Now this is a perfectly valid criticism on all such previous non-theistical arguments as were drawn from an "indication of the process by which the order has been realised;" for in all these previous arguments there was an absence of any physical explanation of the *ultimate* cause of the process contemplated, and so long as this ultimate cause remained obscure, although the evidence of design might by these arguments have been excluded from particular processes, the evidence of design could not be similarly excluded from the ultimate cause of these processes. Thus, for instance, it is doubtless illogical, as

Professor Flint points out, in any Darwinian to argue that because his theory of natural selection supplies him with a natural explanation of the process whereby organisms have been adapted to their surroundings, therefore this process need not itself have been designed. That is to say, in general terms, as insisted upon in the foregoing essay, the discovery of a natural law or orderly process cannot of itself justify the inference that this law or method of orderly procedure is not itself a product of supernatural Intelligence; but, on the contrary, the very existence of such orderly processes, considered only in relation to their products, must properly be regarded as evidence of the best possible kind in favour of supernatural Intelligence, *provided that no natural cause can be suggested as adequate to explain the origin of these processes.* But this is precisely what the persistence of force, considered as a natural cause, must be pronounced as necessarily competent to achieve; for we can clearly see that all these processess obviously must and actually do derive their origin from this one causative principle. And whether or not behind this one causative principle of natural law there exists a still more ultimate cause in the form of a supernatural Intelligence, this is a question altogether foreign to any argument from teleology, seeing that teleology, in so far as it is *teleology*, can only rest upon the observed facts of the cosmos; and if these facts admit of being explained by the action of a single causative principle inherent in the cosmos itself, teleology is not free to assume the action of any causative principle of a more ultimate character. Still, as I have repeatedly insisted, these considerations do not entitle us dogmatically to deny the existence of some such more ultimate principle; all that these considerations do is to remove any rational argument from teleological sources that any such more ultimate principle exists. Therefore I am, of course, quite at one with Professor Flint where he says Professor Huxley "admits that the most thoroughgoing evolutionist must at least assume 'a primordial molecular arrangement of which all the phenomena of the universe are the consequences,' and 'is thereby at the mercy of the theologist, who can defy him to disprove that this primordial molecular arrangement was not intended to involve the phenomena of the universe.' Granting this much, he is logically bound to grant more. If the entire evolution of the universe may have been intended, the several stages of its evolution may have been intended, and they may have been intended for their own sakes as well as for the sake of the collective evolution or its final result." Now that such *may have been* the case, I have been careful to insist in Chapter V.; all I am now concerned with is to show that, in view of the considerations adduced in Chapter IV., there is no longer any evidence to prove, or even to indicate, that such *has been* the case. And with reference to this opportune quotation from Professor Huxley I may remark, that the "thoroughgoing evolutionist" is now no longer "at the mercy of the theologian" to any further extent than that of not being able to disprove a purely metaphysical hypothesis, which is as certainly superfluous, in any scientific sense, as the fundamental data of science are certainly true.

It may seem almost unnecessary to extend this postscript by pursuing further the criticism on Professor Flint's exposition in the light of "a single new reason . . . for the denial of design" which he challenges; but there are nevertheless one or two other points which it seems desirable to consider. Professor Flint writes:—

"M. Comte imagines that he has shown the inference from design, from the order and stability of the solar system, to be unwarranted, when he has pointed out the physical conditions through which that order and stability are secured, and the process by which they have been obtained. . . . Now the assertion that the peculiarities which make the solar system stable and the earth habitable have flowed naturally and necessarily from the simple mutual gravity of the several parts of nebulous matter is one which greatly requires proof, but which has never received it. In saying this, we do not challenge the proof of the nebular theory itself. That theory may or may not be true. We are quite willing to suppose it true—to grant that it has been scientifically established. What we maintain is, that even if we admit unreservedly that the earth and the whole system to which it belongs once existed in a nebulous state, from which they were gradually evolved into their present condition conformably to physical laws, we are in no degree entitled to infer from the admission the conclusion which Comte and others have drawn. The man who fancies that the nebular theory implies that the law of gravitation, or any other physical law, has of itself determined the course of cosmical evolution, so that there is no need for believing in the existence and operation of a divine mind, proves merely that he is not exempt from reasoning very illogically. The solar system could only have been evolved out of its nebulous state into that which it now presents if the nebula possessed a certain size, mass, form, and constitution, if it was neither too fluid nor too tenacious—if its atoms were all numbered, its elements all weighed, its constituents all disposed in due relation to one another; that is to say, only if the nebula was in reality as much a system of order, which Intelligence alone could account for, as the worlds which have been developed from it. The origin of the nebula thus presents itself to reason as a problem which demands solution no less than the origin of the planets. All the properties and laws of the nebula require to be accounted for. What origin are we to give them? It must be either reason or unreason. We may go back as far as we please, but at every step and stage of the regress we must find ourselves confronted with the same question, the same alternative—intelligent purpose or colossal chance."

Now, so far as Comte is here guilty of the fallacy I have already dwelt upon of building a destructive argument upon a demonstration of mere orderly processes in nature, as distinguished from a demonstration of the natural cause of these processes, it is not for me to defend him. All we can say with regard to him in this connection is, that, having a sort of scientific presentiment that if the knowledge of his day were sufficiently advanced it would prove destructive of supernaturalism in the higher and more abstruse provinces of physical speculation, as it had previously proved in the lower and less abstruse of these provinces, Comte allowed his inferences to outrun their legitimate basis. Being necessarily ignorant of the one generating cause of orderly processes in nature, he improperly allowed himself to found conclusions on the basis of these processes alone, which could only be properly founded on the basis of their cause. But freely granting this much to Professor Flint, and the rest of his remarks in this connection will be found, in view of the altered standing of this subject, to be open to amendment. For, in the first place, no one need now resort to the illogical supposition that "the law of gravitation or any other physical law has of itself determined the course of cosmical evolution." What we may argue, and what must be conceded to us, is, that the common substratum of all physical laws was at one time sufficient to produce the simplest physical laws, and that throughout the whole course of evolution this common substratum has always been sufficient to produce the more complex laws in the ascending series of their ever-increasing number and variety. And hence it becomes obvious that the "origin of the nebula" presents a difficulty neither greater nor less than "the origin of the planets," since, "if we may go back as far as we please," we can entertain no *scientific* doubt that we should come to a time, prior even to the nebula, when the substance of the solar system existed merely as such—*i.e.*, in an almost or in a wholly undifferentiated form, the product, no doubt, of endless cycles of previous evolutions and dissolutions of formal differentiations. Therefore, although it is undoubtedly true that "the solar system could only have been evolved out of its nebulous state into that which it now presents if the nebula possessed" those particular attributes which were necessary to the evolution of such a product, this consideration is clearly deprived of all its force from our present point of view. For unless it can be shown that there is some independent reason for believing these particular attributes—which must have been of a more and more simple a character the further we recede in time—to have been miraculously imposed, the analogy is overwhelming that they all progressively arose *by way of natural law*. And if so, the universe which has been thus produced is the only universe in this particular point of space and time which could have been thus produced. That it is an *orderly* universe we have seen *ad nauseam* to be no argument in favour of its having been a *designed* universe, so long as the cause of its order—general laws—can be seen to admit of a natural explanation.

Thus there is clearly nothing to be gained on the side of teleology by going back to the dim and dismal birth of the nebula; for no "thoroughgoing evolutionist" would for one moment entertain the supposition that natural law in the simplest phases of its development partook any more of a miraculous character than it does in its more recent and vastly more complex phases. The absence of knowledge must not be used as equivalent to its presence; and if analogy can be held to justify any inference whatsoever, surely we may conclude with confidence that if existing general laws admit of being conceivably attributed to a natural genesis, the primordial laws of a condensing nebula must have been the same.

There is another passage in Professor Flint's work to which it seems desirable to refer. It begins thus: "There is the law of heredity: like produces like. But why is there such a law? Why does like produce like? . . . . Physical science cannot answer these questions; but that is no reason why they should not both be asked and answered. I can conceive of no other intelligent answer being given to them than that there is a God of wisdom, who designed that the world should be for all ages the abode of life," &c.

Now here we have in another form that same vicious tendency to take refuge in the more obscure cases of physical causation as proofs of supernatural design—the obscurity in this case arising from the *complexity* of the causes and work, as in the former case it arose from their *remoteness* in time. But in both cases the same answer is patent, viz., that although "physical science cannot answer these questions" by pointing out the precise sequence of causes and effects, physical science is nevertheless quite as certain that this precise sequence arises in its last resort from the persistence of force, as she would be were she able to trace the whole process. And therefore, in view of the considerations set forth in Chapter IV. of this work, it is no longer open to Professor Flint or to any other writer logically to assert—"I can conceive of no other intelligent answer being given to" such questions "than that there is a God of wisdom."

The same answer awaits this author's further disquisition on other biological laws, so it is needless to make any further quotations in this connection. But there is one other principle embodied in some of these passages which it seems undesirable to overlook. It is said, for instance, "Natural selection might have had no materials, or altogether insufficient materials, to work with, or the circumstances might have been such that the lowest organisms were the best endowed for the struggle for life. If the earth were covered with water, fish would survive and higher creatures would perish."

Now the principle here embodied—viz., that had the conditions of evolution been other than they were, the results would have been different—is, of course, true; but clearly, on the view that *all* natural laws spring from the persistence of force, no other conditions than those which actually occurred, or are now occurring, could ever have occurred,—the whole course of evolution must have been, in all its phases and in all its processes, an unconditional necessity. But if it is said, How fortunate that the outcome, being unconditionally necessary, has happened to be so good as it is; I answer that the remark is legitimate enough if it is not intended to convey an implication that the general quality of the outcome points to beneficent design as to its cause. Such an implication would not be legitimate, because, in the first place, we have no means of knowing in how many cases, whether in planets, stars, or systems, the course of evolution has failed to produce life and mind—the one known case of this earth, whether or not it is the one success out of millions of abortions, being of necessity the only known case. In how vastly greater a number of cases the course of evolution may have been, so to speak, deflected by some even slight, though strictly necessary, cause from producing self-conscious intelligence, it is impossible to conjecture. But this consideration, be it observed, is not here adduced in order to *disprove* the assertion that telluric evolution has been effected by Intelligence; it is merely adduced to prove that such an assertion cannot rest on the single known result of telluric evolution, so long as an infinite number of the results of evolution elsewhere remain unknown.

And now, lastly, it must be observed that even in the one case with which we are acquainted, the net product of evolution is not such as can of itself point us to *beneficent* design. Professor Flint, indeed, in common with theologians generally, argues that it does. I will therefore briefly criticise his remarks on this subject, believing, as I do, that they form a very admirable illustration of what I conceive to be a general principle—viz., that minds which already believe in the existence of a Deity are, as a rule, not in a position to view this question of beneficence in nature in a perfectly impartial manner. For if the existence of a Deity is presupposed, a mind with any particle of that most noble quality—reverence—will naturally hesitate to draw conclusions that partake of the nature of blasphemy; and therefore, unconsciously perhaps to themselves, they endeavour in various ways to evade the evidence which, if honestly and impartially considered, can scarcely fail to negative the argument from beneficence in the universe.

Professor Flint argues that the "law of over-production," and the consequent struggle for existence, being "the reason why the world is so wonderfully rich in the most varied forms of life," is "a means to an end worthy of Divine Wisdom." "Although involving privation, pain, and conflict, its final result is order and beauty. All the perfections of sentient creatures are represented as due to it. Through it the lion has gained its strength, the deer its speed, and the dog its sagacity. The inference seems natural that these perfections were designed to be attained by it; that this state of struggle was ordained for the sake of the advantages which it is actually seen to produce. The suffering which the conflict involves may indicate that God has made even animals for some higher end than happiness—that he cares for animal perfection as well as for animal enjoyment; but it affords no reason for denying that the ends which the conflict actually serves it was intended to serve."

Now, whatever may be thought of such an argument as an attempted justification of beneficent design already on independent ground believed to exist, it is manifestly no argument at all as establishing any presumption in favour of such design, unless it could be shown that the Deity is so far limited in his power of adapting means to ends that the particular method adopted in this case was the best, all things considered, that he was able to adopt. For supposing the Deity to be, what Professor Flint maintains that he is—viz., omnipotent—and there can be no inference more transparent than that such wholesale suffering, for whatever ends designed, exhibits an incalculably greater deficiency of beneficence in the divine character than that which we know in any, the very worst, of human characters. For let us pause for one moment to think of what suffering in nature means. Some hundreds of millions of years ago some millions of millions of animals must be supposed to have been sentient. Since that time till the present, there must have been millions and millions of generations of millions of millions of individuals. And throughout all this period of incalculable duration, this inconceivable host of sentient organisms have been in a state of unceasing battle, dread, ravin, pain. Looking to the outcome, we find that more than half of the species which have survived the ceaseless struggle are parasitic in their habits, lower and insentient forms of life feasting on higher and sentient forms; we find teeth and talons whetted for slaughter, hooks and suckers moulded for torment—everywhere a reign of terror, hunger, and sickness, with oozing blood and quivering limbs, with gasping breath and eyes of innocence that dimly close in deaths of brutal torture! Is it said that there are compensating enjoyments? I care not to strike the balance; the enjoyments I plainly perceive to be as physically necessary as the pains, and this whether or not evolution is due to design. Therefore all I am concerned with is to show, that if such a state of things is due to "omnipotent design," the omnipotent designer must be concluded, so far as reason can infer, to be non-beneficent. And this it is not difficult to show. When I see a rabbit panting in the iron jaws of a spring-trap, I abhor the devilish nature of the being who, with full powers of realising what pain means, can deliberately employ his noble faculties of invention in contriving a thing so hideously cruel. But if I could believe that there is a being who, with yet higher faculties of thought and knowledge, and with an unlimited choice of means to secure his ends, has contrived untold thousands of mechanisms no less diabolical than a spring-trap; I should call that being a fiend, were all the world besides to call him God. Am I told that this is arrogance? It is nothing of the kind; it is plain morality, and to say otherwise would be to hide our eyes from murder because we dread the Murderer. Am I told that I am not competent to judge the purposes of the Almighty? I answer that if these are *purposes*, I *am* able to judge of them so far as I can see; and if I am expected to judge of his purposes when they appear to be beneficent, I am in consistency obliged also to judge of them when they appear to be malevolent. And it can be no possible extenuation of the latter to point to the "final result" as "order and beauty," so long as the means adopted by the "*Omnipotent* Designer" are known to have been so revolting. All that we could legitimately assert in this case would be, that so far as observation can extend, "he cares for animal perfection" *to the exclusion of* "animal enjoyment," and even to the *total disregard* of animal suffering. But to assert this would merely be to deny beneficence as an attribute of God.

The dilemma, therefore, which Epicurus has stated with great lucidity, and which Professor Flint quotes, appears to me so obvious as scarcely to require statement. The dilemma is, that, looking to the facts of organic nature, theists must abandon their belief, either in the divine omnipotence, or in the divine beneficence. And yet, such is the warping effect of preformed beliefs on the mind, that even so candid a writer as Professor Flint can thus write of this most obvious truth:—

"The late Mr. John Stuart Mill, for no better reason than that nature sometimes drowns men and burns them, and that childbirth is a painful process, maintained that God could not possibly be infinite. I shall not say what I think of the shallowness and self-conceit displayed by such an argument. What it proves is not the finiteness of God, but the littleness of man. The mind of man never shows itself so small as when it tries to measure the attributes and limit the greatness of its Creator."

But the argument—or rather the truism—in question is an attempt to do neither the one nor the other; it simply asserts the patent fact that, if God is omnipotent, and so had an unlimited choice of means whereby to accomplish the ends of "animal perfection," "animal enjoyment," and the rest; then the fact of his having chosen to adopt the means which he has adopted is a fact which is wholly incompatible with his beneficence. And on the other hand, if he is beneficent, the fact of his having adopted these means in order that the sum of ultimate enjoyment might exceed the sum of concomitant pain, is a fact which is wholly incompatible with his omnipotence. To a man who already believes, on independent grounds, in an omnipotent and beneficent Deity, it is no doubt possible to avoid facing this dilemma, and to rest content with the assumption that, in a sense beyond the reach of human reason, or even of human conception, the two horns of this dilemma must be united in some transcendental reconciliation; but if a man undertakes to reason on the subject at all, as he must and ought when the question is as to the *existence* of such a Deity, then clearly he has no alternative but to allow that the dilemma is a hopeless one. With inverted meaning, therefore, may we quote Professor Flint's words against himself:—" The mind of man never shows itself so small as when it tries to measure the attributes . . . . of its Creator;" for certainly, if Professor Flint's usually candid mind has had a Creator, it nowhere displays the "littleness" of prejudice in so marked a degree as it does when "measuring his attributes."

Thus in a subsequent chapter he deals at greater length with this difficulty of the apparent failure of beneficence in nature, arguing, in effect, that as pain and suffering "serve many good ends" in the way of warning animals of danger to life, &c., therefore we ought to conclude that, if we could see farther, we should see pain and suffering to be unmitigated good, or nearly so. Now this argument, as I have previously said, may possible be admissible as between Christians or others who *already* believe in the existence and in the beneficence of God; but it is only the blindest prejudice which can fail to perceive that the argument is quite without relevancy when the question is as to the *evidences* of such existence and the *evidences* of such character. For where the *fact* of such an existence and character is the question in dispute, it clearly can be no argument to state its bare assumption by saying that if we knew more of nature we should find the relative preponderance of good over evil to be immeasurably greater than that which we now perceive. The platform of argument on which the question of "Theism" must be discussed is that of the observable Cosmos; and if, as Dr. Flint is constrained to admit, there is a fearful spectacle of misery presented by this Cosmos, it becomes mere question-begging to gloss over this aspect of the subject by any vague assumption that the misery must have some unobservable ends of so transcendentally beneficent a nature, that were they known they would justify the means. Indeed, this kind of discussion seems to me worse than useless for the purposes which the Professor has in view; for it only serves by contrast to throw out into stronger relief the natural and the unstrained character of the adverse interpretation of the facts. According to this adverse interpretation, sentiency has been evolved by natural selection to secure the benefits which are pointed out by Professor Flint; and therefore the fact of this, its cause, having been a *mindless* cause, clearly implies that the *restriction* of pain and suffering cannot be an active principle, or a *vera causa*, as between species and species, though it must be such within the limits of the same organism, and to a lesser extent within the limits of the same species. And this is just what we find to be the case. Therefore, without the need of resorting to wholly arbitrary assumptions concerning transcendental reconciliations between apparently needless suffering and a supposed almighty beneficence, the non-theistic hypothesis is saved by merely opening our eyes to the observable facts around us, and there seeing that pain and misery, alike in the benefits which they bring and in the frightful excesses which they manifest, play just that part in nature which this hypothesis would lead us to expect.

Therefore, to sum up these considerations on physical suffering, the case between a theist and a sceptic as to the question of divine beneficence is seen to be a case of extreme simplicity. The theist believes in such beneficence by purposely concealing from his mind all adverse evidence —feeling, on the one side, that to entertain the doubt to which this evidence points would be to hold dalliance with blasphemy, and, on the other side, that the subject is of so transcendental a nature that, in view of so great a risk, it is better to avoid impartial reasoning upon it. A sceptic, on the other hand, is under no such obligation to preconceived ideas, and is therefore free to draw unbiassed inferences as to the character of God, if he exists, to the extent which such character is indicated by the sphere of observable nature. And, as I have said, when the subject is so viewed, the inference is unavoidable that, so far as human reason can penetrate, God, if he exists, must either be non-infinite in his resources, or non-beneficent in his designs. Therefore it is evident that when the *being* of God, as distinguished from his *character*, is the subject in dispute, Theism can gain nothing by an appeal to evidences of *beneficent* designs. If such evidences were unequivocal, then indeed the argument which they would establish to an intelligent cause of nature would be almost irresistible; for the fact of the external world being in harmony with the moral nature of man would be unaccountable except on the supposition of both having derived their origin from a common *moral* source; and morality implies intelligence. But as it is, all the so-called evidence of divine beneficence in nature is, without any exception of a kind that is worthless as proving *design*; for all the facts admit of being explained equally well on the supposition of their having been due to purely physical processes, acting through the various biological laws which we are now only beginning to understand. And further than this, so far are these facts from proving the existence of a moral cause, that, in view of the alternative just stated, they even ground a positive argument to its negation. For, as we have seen, all these facts are just of such a kind as we should expect to be the facts, on the supposition of their having been due to natural causes—*i.e.*, causes which could have had no moral solicitude for animal happiness as such. Let us now, in conclusion, dwell on this antithesis at somewhat greater length.

If natural selection has played any large share in the process of organic evolution, it is evident that animal enjoyment, being an important factor in this natural cause, must always have been furthered *to the extent in which it was necessary for the adaptation of organisms to their environment* that it should. And such we invariably find to be the limits within which animal enjoyments *are* confined. On the other hand, so long as the adaptations in question are not complete, so long must more or less of suffering be entailed—the capacity for suffering, as for enjoyment, being no doubt itself a product of natural selection. But as all specific types are perpetually struggling together, it is manifest that the competition must prevent any considerable number of types from becoming so far adapted to their environment of other types as to become exempt from suffering as a result of this competition. There being no one integrating cause of an intelligent or moral nature to supply the conditions of happiness to each organic type without the misery of this competition, such happiness as animals have is derived from the heavy expenditure of pain suffered by themselves and by their ancestry.

Thus, whether we look to animal pleasures or to animal pains, the result is alike just what we should expect to find on the supposition of these pleasures and pains having been due to necessary and physical, as distinguished from intelligent and moral, antecedents; for how different is that which is from that which might have been! Not only might beneficent selection have eliminated the countless species of parasites which now destroy the health and happiness of all the higher organisms; not only might survival of the fittest, in a moral sense, have determined that rapacious and carnivorous animals should yield their places in the world to harmless and gentle ones; not only might life have been without sickness and death without pain;—but how might the exigences and the welfare of species have been consulted by the structures and the habits of one another! But no! Amid all the millions of mechanisms and habits in organic nature, all of which are so beautifully adapted to the needs of the species presenting them, there is *no single instance* of any mechanism or habit occurring in one species for the exclusive benefit of another species — although, as we should expect on the non-theistic theory, there are some comparatively few cases of a mechanism or a habit which is of benefit to its possessor being also utilised by other species. Yet, on the beneficent-design theory, it is impossible to understand why, when all mechanisms and habits in the same species are invariably correlated for the benefit of that species, there should never be any such correlation between mechanisms and habits of different species. For how magnificent, how sublime a display of supreme beneficence would nature have afforded if all her sentient animals had been so inter-related as to minister to each other's happiness! Organic species might then have been likened to a countless multitude of voices, all singing to their Creator in one harmonious psalm of praise. But, as it is, we see no vestige of such correlation; every species is for itself, and for itself alone—an outcome of the always and everywhere fiercely raging struggle for life.

So much, then, for the case of *physical* evil; but Dr. Flint also treats of the case of *moral* evil. Let us see what this well-equipped writer can make of this old problem in the present year of grace. He says—" But it will be objected, could not God have made moral creatures who would be certain always to choose what is right, always to acquiesce in His holy will? . . . Well, far be it from me to deny that God could have originated a sinless moral system. . . . But if questioned as to why He has not done better, I feel no shame in confessing my ignorance. It seems to me that when you have resolved the problem of the origin of moral evil into the question, Why has God not originated a moral universe in which the lowest moral being would be as excellent as the archangels are? you have at once shown it to be *speculatively incapable of solution* [italics mine], and practically without importance [!]. The question is one which would obviously give rise to another, Why has God not created only moral beings as much superior to the archangels as they are superior to the lowest Australian aborigines? But no complete answer can be given to a question which may be followed by a series of similar questions to which there is no end. We have, besides, neither the facts nor the faculties to answer such questions."[1]

Now I confess that this argument presents to my mind more of subtlety than sense. I had previously imagined that the archangels were supposed to enjoy a condition of moral existence which might fairly be thought to remove them from any association with that of the Australian aborigines. But as this question is one that belongs to Divinity, I am here quite prepared to bow to Professor Flint's authority—hoping, however, that he is prepared to take the responsibility should the archangels ever care to accuse me of calumny. But, as a logician, I must be permitted to observe, that if I ask, Why am I not better than I am? it is no answer to tell me, Because' the archangels are not better than they are. For aught that I know to the contrary, the archangels may be morally *perfect*—as an

[1] Op. cit., pp. 255-257.

authority in such matters has told us that even "just men" may become,—and therefore, for aught that I know to the contrary, Professor Flint's regress of moral degrees *ad infinitum*, may be an ontological absurdity. But granting, for the sake of argument, that archangels fall infinitely short of moral perfection, and I should only be able to see in the fact a hopeless aggravation of my previous difficulty. If it is hard to reconcile the supreme goodness of God with the moral turpitude of man, much more would it be hard to do so if his very angels are depraved. Therefore, if the reasonable question which I originally put "may be followed by a series of similar questions to which there is no end," the goodness of God must simply be pronounced a delusion. For the question which I originally put was no mere flimsy question of a stupidly unreal description. My own moral depravity is a matter of painful certainty to me, and I want to know why, if there is a God of infinite power and goodness, he should have made me thus. And in answer I am told that my question is "practically without importance," because there may be an endless series of beings who, in their several degrees, are in a similar predicament to myself. Perhaps they are; but if so, the moral evil with which I am directly acquainted is made all the blacker by the fact that it is thus but a drop in an infinite ocean of moral imperfection. When, therefore, Professor Flint goes on to say, "We ought to be content if we can show that what God has done is wise and right, and not perplex ourselves as to why He has not done an infinity of other things," I answer, Most certainly; but *can* we show that what God has done is wise and right? Unquestionably not. That what he has done *may* be wise and right, could we see his whole scheme of things, no careful thinker will deny; but to suppose it can be *shown* that he has done this, is an instance of purblind fanaticism which is most startling in a work on *Theism*. "The best world, *we may be assured*, that our fancies can feign, would in reality be far inferior to the world God has made, whatever imperfections we may think we see in it." Are we reading a sermon on the datum "God is love"? No; but a work on the questions, Is there a God? and, if so, Is he a God of love? And yet the work is written by a man who evidently tries to argue fairly. What shall we say of the despotism of preformed beliefs? May we not say at least this much—that those who endeavour to reconcile their theories of divine goodness with the facts of human evil might well appropriate to themselves the words above quoted, "We have neither the facts nor the faculties to answer such questions"? For the "facts" indeed are absent, and the "faculties" of impartial thought must be absent also, if this obvious truth cannot be seen—that "these questions" only derive their "speculatively unanswerable" character from the rational falsity of the manner by which it is sought to answer them. The "facts" of our moral nature, so far as honest reason can perceive, belie the hypothesis of Theism; and although the "faculties" of man may be forced by prejudice into an acceptance of contradictory propositions, the truth is obvious that only by the hypothesis of Evolution can that old-tied knot be cut—the Origin of Evil. The form of Theism for which Dr. Flint is arguing is the current form, viz., that there is a God who combines in himself the attributes of *infinite* power and *perfect* goodness—a God at once *omnipotent* and *wholly* moral. But, in view of the fact that moral evil exists in man, the proposition that God is omnipotent and the proposition that he is wholly moral become contradictory; and therefore the fact of moral evil can only be met, either by abandoning one or other of these propositions, or by altogether rejecting the hypothesis of Theism.

III.

THE SPECULATIVE STANDING OF MATERIALISM.

As a continuation of my criticism on Mr. Fiske's views, I think it is desirable to add a few words concerning the speculative annihilation with which he supposes Mr. Spencer's doctrines to have visited Materialism. Of course it is a self-evident truism that the doctrine of Relativity is destructive of Materialism, if by Materialism we mean a theory which ignores that doctrine. In other words, the doctrine of Relativity, if accepted, clearly excludes the doctrine that Matter, *as known phenomenally*, is at all likely to be a true representative of whatever *thing-in-itself* it may be that constitutes Mind. But this position is fully established by the doctrine of Relativity alone, and is therefore not in the least affected, either by way of confirmation or otherwise, by Mr. Spencer's extended doctrine of the Unknowable—it being only because the latter doctrine presupposes the doctrine of Relativity that it is exclusive of Materialism in the sense which has just been stated. So far, therefore, Mr. Spencer's writings cannot be held to have any special bearing on the doctrine of Materialism. Such a special bearing is only exerted by these writings when they proceed to show that "it seems an imaginable possibility that units of external force may be identical in nature with the units of the force known as feeling." Let us then ascertain how far it is true that the argument already quoted, and which leads to this conclusion, is utterly destructive of Materialism.

In the first place, I may observe that this argument differs in several instructive particulars from the anti-materialistic argument of Locke, which we have already had occasion to consider. For while Locke erroneously imagined that the test of inconceivability is of equivalent value *wherever* it is applied, save only where it conflicts with preconceived ideas on the subject of Theism (see Appendix A.), Spencer, of course, is much too careful a thinker to fall into so obvious a fallacy. But again, it is curious to observe that in the anti-materialistic argument of Spencer the test of inconceivability is used in a manner the precise opposite of that in which it is used in the anti-materialistic argument of Locke. For while the ground of Locke's argument is that Materialism must be untrue because it is inconceivable that Matter (and Force) should be of a psychical nature; the ground of Spencer's argument is that what we know as Force (and Matter) may *not* inconceivably be of a psychical nature. For my own part, I think that Spencer's argument is, psychologically speaking, the more valid of the two; but nevertheless I think that, logically speaking, it is likewise invalid to a perceptibly great, and to a further indefinite, degree. For the argument sets out with the reflection that we can only know Matter and Force as symbols of consciousness, while we know consciousness directly, and therefore that we can go further in conceivably translating Matter and Force into terms of Mind than *vice versa*. And this is true, but it does not therefore follow that the truth is more likely to lie in the direction that thought can most easily travel. For although I am at one with Mr. Spencer, whom Mr. Fiske follows, in regarding his test of truth—viz., inconceivability of a negation—as the most *ultimate* test within our reach, I cannot agree with him that in this particular case it is the most *trustworthy* test within our reach. I cannot do so because the reflection is forced upon me that, "as the terms which are contemplated in this particular case are respectively the highest abstractions of objective and of subjective existence, the test of truth in question is neutralised by directly encountering the inconceivable relation that exists between subject and object." Or, in other words, as before stated, "*whatever* the cause of Mind may be, we can clearly perceive it to be a subjective necessity of the case that, in ultimate analysis, we should find it more easy to conceive of this cause as resembling Mind—the only entity of which we are directly conscious—than to conceive of it as any other entity of which we are only indirectly conscious." When, therefore, Mr. Spencer argues that "it is impossible to interpret inner existence in terms of outer existence," while it is not so impossible to interpret outer existence in terms of inner existence, the fact is merely what we should in any case expect *à priori* to be the fact, and therefore as a fact it is not a very surprising discovery *à posteriori*. So that when Mr. Fiske proceeds to make this fact the basis of his argument, that because we can more conceivably regard objective existence as like in kind to subjective existence than conversely, therefore we should conclude that there is a corresponding probability in favour of the more conceivable proposition, I demur to his argument. For, fully accepting the fact on which the argument rests, and it seems to me, in view of what I have said, that the latter assigns an altogether disproportionate value to the test of inconceivability in this case. Far from endowing this test with so great an authority in this case, I should regard it not only as perceptibly of very small validity, but, as I have said, invalid to a degree which we have no means of ascertaining. If it be asked, What other gauge of probability can we have in this matter other than such a direct appeal to consciousness? I answer, that this appeal being here *à priori* invalid, we are left to fall back upon the formal probability which is established by an application of scientific canons to objective phenomena. (See footnote in § 14.) For, be it carefully observed, Mr. Spencer, and his disciple Mr. Fiske, are not idealists. Were this the case, of course the test of an immediate appeal to consciousness would be to them the only test available. But, on the contrary, as all the world knows, Mr. Spencer asserts the existence of an unknown Reality, of which all phenomena are the manifestations. Consequently, what we call Force and Matter are, according to this doctrine, phenomenal manifestations of this objective Reality. That is to say, for aught that we can know, Force and Matter may be anything within the whole range of the possible; and the only limitation that can be assigned to them is, that they are modes of existence which are independent of, or objective to, our individual consciousness, but which are uniformly translated into consciousness as Force and Matter. Now it does not signify one iota for the purposes of Materialism whether these our symbolical representations of Force and Matter are accurate or inaccurate representations of their corresponding realities,—unless, of course, some *independent* reason could be shown for supposing that in their reality they resemble Mind. Call Force x and Matter y, and so long as we are agreed that x and y are *objective realities which are uniformly translated into consciousness as Force and Matter*, the materialistic deductions remain unaffected by this mere change in our terminology; these essential facts are allowed to remain substantially as before, namely, that there is an external something or external somethings—Matter and Force, or x and y—which themselves display no observable tokens of consciousness, but which are invariably associated with consciousness in a highly distinctive manner.

I dwell at length upon this subject, because although Mr. Spencer himself does not appear to attach much weight to his argument, Mr. Fiske, as we have seen, elevates it into a basis for "Cosmic Theism." Yet so far is this argument from "ruling out," as Mr. Fiske asserts, the essential doctrine of Materialism—*i.e.*, the doctrine that what we know as Mind is an effect of certain collocations and distributions of *what we know* as Matter and Force—that the argument might be employed with almost the same degree of effect, or absence of effect, to disprove any instance of recognised causation. Thus, for example, the doctrine of Materialism is no more "ruled out" by the reflection that what we cognise as cerebral matter is only cognised relatively, than would the doctrine of chemical equivalents be "ruled out" by the parallel reflection that what we cognise as chemical elements are only cognised relatively. I say advisedly, "with *almost* the same degree of effect," because, to be strictly accurate, we ought not altogether to ignore the indefinitely slender presumption which Mr. Spencer's subjective test of inconceivability establishes on the side of Spiritualism, as against the objective evidence of causation on the side of Materialism. As this is an important subject, I will be a little more explicit. We are agreed that Force and Matter are entities external to consciousness, of which we can possess only symbolical knowledge. Therefore, as we have said, Force and Matter may be anything within the whole range of the possible. But we know that Mind is a possible entity, while we have no certain knowledge of any other possible entity. Hence we are justified in saying, It is possible that Force and Matter may be identical with the only entity which we know as certainly possible; but forasmuch as we do not know the sum of possible entities, we have no means of calculating the chances there are that what we know as Force and Matter are identical in nature with Mind. Still, that there is *a* chance we cannot dispute; all we can assert is, that we are unable to determine its value, and that it would be a mistake to suppose we can do so, even in the lowest degree, by Mr. Spencer's test of inconceivability. Nevertheless, the fact that there is such a chance renders it in some indeterminate degree more probable that what we know as Force and Matter are identical with what we know as Mind, than that what we know as oxygen and hydrogen are identical with what we know as water. So that to this extent the essential doctrine of Materialism is "ruled out" in a further degree by the philosophy of the Unknowable than is the chemical doctrine of equivalents. But, of course, this indefinite possibility of what we know as Force and Matter being identical with what we know as Mind does not neutralise, in any determinable degree, the considerations whereby Materialism in its present shape infers that what we know as Force and Matter are probably distinct from what we know as Mind.

But I see no reason why Materialism should be restricted to this "its present shape." Even if we admit to the fullest extent the validity of Mr. Spencer's argument, and conclude with Professor Clifford as a matter of probability that "the universe consists entirely of Mind-stuff," I do not see that the admission would affect Materialism in any essential respect. For here again the admission would amount to little else, so far as Materialism is directly concerned, than a change of terminology: instead of calling objective existence "Matter," we call it "Mind-stuff." I say "to *little* else," because no doubt in one particular there is here some change introduced in the speculative standing of the subject. So long as Matter and Mind, x and y, are held to be antithetically opposed in substance, so long must Materialism suppose that a connection of *causality* subsists between the two, such that the former substance is *produced* in some unaccountable way by the latter. But when Matter and Mind, x and y, are supposed to be identical in substance, the need for any additional supposition as to a causal connection is excluded. But unless we hold, what seems to me an uncalled-for opinion, that the essential feature of Materialism consists in a postulation of a causal connection between x and y, it would appear that the only effect of supposing x and y to be really but one substance z, must be that of *strengthening* the essential doctrine of Materialism—the doctrine, namely, that conscious intellectual existence is *necessarily* associated with that form of existence which we know phenomenally as Matter and Motion. If it is true that a "a moving molecule of inorganic matter does not possess mind or consciousness, but it possesses a small piece of Mind-stuff," then assuredly the central position of Materialism is shown to be impregnable. For while it remains as true as ever that mind and consciousness can only emerge when what we know phenomenally as " Matter takes the complex form of a living brain," we have abolished the necessity for assuming even a causal connection between the substance of what we know phenomenally as Matter and the substance of what we know phenomenally as Mind: we have found that, in the last resort, the phenomenal connection between what we know as Matter and what we know as Mind is actually even more intimate than a connection of causality; we have found that it is a substantial identity.

To sum up this discussion. We have considered the bearing of modern speculation on the doctrine of Materialism in three successive stages of argument. First, we had to consider the bearing on Materialism of the simple doctrine of Relativity. Here we saw that Materialism was only affected to the extent of being compelled to allow that what we know as Matter and Motion are not known as they are in themselves. But we also saw that, as the inscrutable realities are uniformly translated into consciousness as Matter and Motion, it still remains as true as ever that *what we know* as Matter and Motion may be the causes of what we know as Mind. Even, therefore, if the supposition of causality is taken to be an essential feature of Materialism, Materialism would be in no wise affected by substituting for the words Matter and Motion the symbols x and y.

The second of the three stages consisted in showing that Mr. Spencer's argument as to the possible identity of Force and Feeling is not in itself sufficient to overthrow the doctrine that what we know as Matter and Motion may be the cause of what we know as Mind. For the mere fact of its being more *conceivable* that units of Force should resemble units of Feeling than conversely, is no warrant for concluding that in reality any corresponding probability obtains. The test of conceivability, although the most ultimate test that is available, is here rendered vague and valueless by the *à priori* consideration that *whatever* the cause of Mind may be (if it has a cause), we must find it more easy to conceive of this cause as resembling Mind than to conceive of it as resembling any other entity of which we are only conscious indirectly.

Lastly, in the third place, we saw that even if Mr. Spencer's argument were fully subscribed to, and Mind in its substantial essence were conceded to be causeless, the central position of Materialism would still remain unaffected. For Mr. Spencer does not suppose that his "units of Force" are themselves endowed with consciousness, any more than Professor Clifford supposes his "moving molecules of inorganic matter" to be thus endowed. So that the only change which these possibilities, even if conceded to be actualities, produce in the speculative standing of Materialism, is to show that the raw material of consciousness, instead of requiring to be *caused* by other substances—Matter and Force, x and y,—occurs ready made as those substances. But the essential feature of Materialism remains untouched—namely, that what we know as Mind is dependent (whether by way of causality or not is immaterial) on highly complex forms of *what we know* as Matter, in association with highly peculiar distributions of *what we know* as Force.

IV.

THE FINAL MYSTERY OF THINGS.

SOME physicists are inclined to dispute the fundamental proposition on which the whole of Mr. Spencer's system of philosophy may be said to rest — the proposition, namely, that the fact of the "persistence of force" constitutes the ultimate basis of science. For my own part, I cannot but believe that any disagreement on this matter only arises from some want of mutual understanding; and, therefore, in order to anticipate any criticisms to which the present work may be open on this score, I append this explanatory note.

I readily grant that the term "persistence of force" is not a happy one, seeing that the word "force," as used by physicists, does not at the present time convey the full meaning which Mr. Spencer desires it to convey. But I think that any impartial physicist will be prepared to admit that, in the present state of his science, we are entitled to conclude that energy of position is merely the result of energy of motion; or, in other words, that potential energy is merely an expression of the fact that the universe, as a whole, is replete with actual energy, whose essential characteristic is that it is indestructible. And this may be concluded without committing ourselves to any particular theory as to the physical explanation of gravity; all we need assert is, that in some way or other gravity is the result of ubiquitous energy. And this, it seems to me, we must assert, or else conclude that gravity can never admit of a physical explanation. For all that we mean by a physical explanation is the proved establishment of an equation between two quantities of energy; so that if energy of position does not admit of being interpreted in terms of energy of motion, we must conclude that it does not admit of being interpreted at all—at least not in any physical sense.

Throughout the foregoing essays, therefore, I have assumed that all forms of energy are but relatively varying expressions of the same fact—the fact, namely, which Mr. Spencer means to express when he says that force is persistent. And it seems to me almost needless to show that this fact is really the basis of all science. For unless this fact is assumed as a postulate, not only would scientific inquiry become impossible, but all experience would become chaotic. The physicist could not prosecute his researches unless he presupposed that the forces which he measures are of a permanent nature, any more than could the chemist prosecute his researches unless he presupposed that the materials which he estimates by energy-units are likewise of a permanent nature. And similarly with all the other sciences, as well as with every judgment in our daily experience. If, therefore, any one should be hypercritical enough to dispute the position that the doctrine of the conservation of energy constitutes the "ultimate datum" of science, I think it will be enough to observe that if this is *not* the "ultimate datum" of science, science can have no "ultimate datum" at all. For any datum more ultimate than permanent existence is manifestly impossible, while any such datum as non-permanent existence would clearly render science impossible. Even, therefore, if such hypercriticism had a valid basis of apparently adverse fact whereon to stand, I should feel myself justified in neglecting it on *à priori* grounds; but the only basis on which such hypercriticism can rest is, not the knowledge of any adverse facts, but the ignorance of certain facts which we must either conclude to be facts or else conclude that science can have no ultimate datum whereon to rest. In the foregoing essays, therefore, I have not scrupled to maintain that the ultimate datum of science is destructive of teleology as a scientific argument for Theism; because, unless we deny the possibility of any such ultimate datum, and so land ourselves in hopeless scepticism, we must conclude that there can be no datum more ultimate than this—Permanent Existence; and this is just the datum which we have seen to be destructive of teleology as a scientific argument for Theism.

It may be well to point out that from this ultimate datum of science—or rather, let us say, of experience—there follows a deductive explanation of the law of causation. For this law, when stripped of all the metaphysical corruptions with which it has been so cumbersomely clothed, simply means that a given collocation of antecedents unconditionally produces a certain consequent. But this fact, otherwise stated, amounts to nothing more than a re-statement of the ultimate datum of experience—the fact that energy is indestructible. For if this latter fact be granted, it is obvious that the so-called law of causation follows as a deductive necessity—or rather, as I have said, that this law becomes but another way of expressing the same fact. This is obvious if we reflect that the only means we have of ascertaining that energy is *not* destructible, is by observing that similar antecedents *do* invariably determine similar consequents. It is as a vast induction from all those particular cases of sequence-changes which collectively we call causation that we conclude energy to be indestructible. And, obversely, having concluded energy to be indestructible, we can plainly see that in any particular cases of its manifestation in sequence-phenomena, the unconditional resemblance between effects due to similar causes which is formulated by the law of causation is merely the direct expression of the fact which we had previously concluded. It seems to me, therefore, that the old-standing question concerning the nature of causation ought now properly to be considered as obsolete. Doubtless there will long remain a sort of hereditary tendency in metaphysical minds to look upon cause-connection as "a mysterious tie" between antecedent and consequent; but henceforth there is no need for scientific minds to regard this "tie" as "mysterious" in any other sense than the existence of energy is "mysterious." To state the law of causation is merely to state the fact that energy is indestructible.

And from this there also arises at once the explanation and the justification of our belief in the uniformity of nature. If energy is, in its relation to us, ubiquitous and persistent, it clearly follows that in all its manifestations which collectively we call nature, similar preceding manifestations must always determine similar succeeding manifestations; for otherwise the energy concerned would require on one or on both of the occasions, either to have become augmented by creation, or dissipated by annihilation. Thus our belief in the uniformity of nature, as in the validity of the law of causation, is merely an expression of our belief in the ubiquitous and indestructible character of energy.

Such being the case, we may fairly conclude that all these old-standing "mysteries" are now merged in the one mystery of existence. And deeper than this it is manifestly impossible that they can be merged; for it is manifestly impossible that Existence in the abstract can ever admit of what we call explanation. Hence we can clearly see that, in a scientific sense, there must always remain a final mystery of things. But although we can thus see that, from the very meaning of what we call explanation, it follows that at the base of all our explanations there must lie a great Inexplicable, I think that the mystery of Existence in the abstract may be rendered less appalling if we reflect that, as opposed to Existence, there is only one logical alternative—Non-existence. Supposing, then, our physical explanations to have reached their highest limits by resolving all modes of Existence into one mode—force, matter, life, and mind, being shown but different manifestations of the same Infinite Existence—the final mystery of things would then become resolved into the simple question, Why is there Existence?—Why is there not Nothing?

Let us then first ask, What is "Nothing"? Is it a mere word, which presents no meaning as corresponding to any objective reality, or has the word a meaning notwithstanding its being an inconceivable one? Or, otherwise phrased, is Nothing possible or impossible? Now, although in ordinary conversation it is generally taken for granted that Nothing is possible, there is certainly no more ground for this supposition than there is for its converse—viz., that Nothing is merely a word which signifies the negation of possibility. For analysis will show that the choice between these two counter-suppositions can only be made in the presence of knowledge which is necessarily absent—the knowledge whether the universe of Existence is finite or infinite. If the universe as a whole is finite, the word Nothing would stand as a symbol to denote an unthinkable blank of which a finite universe is the content. And forasmuch as Something and Nothing would then become actual, as distinguished from nominal correlatives, we could have no guarantee that, in an absolute or transcendental sense, it may not be possible, although it is inconceivable, for Something to become Nothing or Nothing Something. Hence, if Existence is finite, No-existence becomes possible; and the doctrine of the indestructibility of Existence becomes, for aught that we can tell, of a merely relative signification. But, on the other hand, if Existence is infinite, No-existence becomes impossible; and the doctrine of the indestructibility of Existence becomes, in a logical sense, of an absolute signification. For it is manifest that if the universe of Existence is without end in space and time, the possibility of No-existence is of necessity excluded, and the word

"Nothing" thus becomes a mere negation of possibility.[1]

Thus, if it be conceded that the universe as a whole is infinite both in space and time, the concession amounts to an abolition of the final mystery of things. For all that we mean by a mystery is something that requires an explanation, and the whole of the final mystery of things is therefore embodied in the question, "Why is there Existence?—Why is there not Nothing?" But if the universe of Existence be conceded infinite, this question is sufficiently met by the answer, "Because Existence is, and Nothing is not." If it is retorted, But this is no real answer; I reply, It is as real as the question. For to ask, Why is there Existence? is, upon the supposition which has been conceded, equivalent to asking, Why is the possible possible? And if such questions cannot be answered, it is scarcely right to say that on this account they embody a mystery; because the questions are really not rational questions, and therefore the fact of their not admitting of any rational answer cannot be held to show that the questions embody any rational mystery. That there *is* a

---

[1] Let it be observed that there is a distinction between what I may call substantial and formal existence. Thus there is no doubt that flowers as flowers perish, or become non-existent; but the substances of which they were composed persist. And, in this connection, I may here point out that if the universe is infinite in space and time, the universe as a whole would present substantial existence as standing out of relation to space and time, whereas innumerable portions of the universe present only formal existences, because standing in relation both to space and time. Thus, for instance, the solar system, as a solar system, must have an end in time as it has a boundary in space; but as the substance of which it consists will not become extinguished by the extinction of the system, it may not now stand in any real relation to what we call space and time. I am inclined to think that it is upon the idea of non-existence in this formal sense that we construct a pseud-idea of non-existence in a substantial sense; but it is evident that if the universe as a whole is absolute, this pseud-idea must represent an impossibility. And from this it follows, that if existence is infinite in space and time, every *quantum* of it with which our experience comes into relation must present, as its essential quality, that quality which we find to be presented by the substance of things—the quality, that is, of persistence.

rational mystery, in the sense of there being something which can never be *explained*, I do not dispute; all I assert is, that this mystery is inexplicable only *because there is nothing to explain;* the mystery being ultimate, to ask for an explanation of that which, being ultimate, requires no explanation, is irrational. Or, to state the case in another way, if it is asked, Why is there not Nothing? it is a sufficient answer, on supposition of the universe being infinite, to say, Because Nothing is nothing; it is merely a word which presents no meaning, and which, so far as anything can be conceived to the contrary, never can present any meaning.

The above discussion has proceeded on the supposition of Existence being infinite; but practically the same result would follow on the counter-supposition of Existence being finite. For although in this case, as we have seen, Non-entity would be included within the range of possibility, it would still be no more conceivable as such than is Entity; and hence the question, Why is there not Nothing? would still be irrational, seeing that, even if the possibility which the question supposes were realised, it would in no wise tend to explain the mystery of Something. And even if it could, the final mystery would not be thus excluded; it would merely be transferred from the mystery of Existence to the mystery of Non-existence. Thus under every conceivable supposition we arrive at the same termination —viz., that in the last resort there must be a final mystery, which, as forming the basis of all possible explanations, cannot itself receive any explanation, and which therefore is really not, in any proper sense of the term, a mystery at all. It is merely a fact which itself requires no explanation, because it is a fact than which none can be more ultimate. So that even if we suppose this ultimate fact to be an Intelligent Being, it is clearly impossible that he should be able to *explain* his own existence, since the possibility of any such explanation would imply that his existence could not be ultimate. In the sense, therefore, of not admitting of any explanation, his existence would require to be a mystery to himself, rendering it impossible for him to state anything further with regard to it than this—" I am that I am."

I do not doubt that this way of looking at the subject will be deemed unsatisfactory at first sight, because it seems to be, as it were, a merely logical way of cheating our intelligence out of an intuitively felt justification for its own curiosity in this matter. But the fault really lies in this intuitive feeling of justification not being itself justifiable. For this particular question, it will be observed, differs from all other possible questions with which the mind has to deal. All other questions being questions concerning manifestations of existence presupposed as existing, it is perfectly legitimate to seek for an explanation of one series of manifestations in another—*i.e.*, to refer a less known group to a group better known. But the case is manifestly quite otherwise when, having merged one group of manifestations into another group, and this into another for an indefinite number of stages, we suddenly make a leap to the last possible stage and ask, " Into what group are we to merge the basis of all our previous groups, and of all groups which can possibly be formed in the future ? How are we to classify that which contains all possible classes ? Where are we to look for an explanation of Existence ?" When thus clearly stated, the question is, as I have said, manifestly irrational; but the point with which I am now concerned is this—When in plain reason the question is *seen* to be irrational, why in intuitive sentiment should it not be *felt* to be so ? The answer, I think, is, that the interrogative faculty being usually occupied with questions which admit of rational answers, we acquire a sort of intellectual habit of presupposing every wherefore to have a therefore, and thus, when eventually we arrive at the last of all possible wherefores, which itself supplies the basis of all possible therefores, we fail at first to recognise the exceptional character of our position. We fail at first to perceive that, from the very nature of this particular case, our wherefore is deprived of the rational meaning which it had in all the previous cases, where the possibility of a corresponding therefore was presupposed. And failing fully to perceive this truth, our organised habit of expecting an answer to our question asserts itself, and we experience the same sense of intellectual unrest in the presence of this wholly meaningless and absurd question, as we experience in the presence of questions significant and rational.

THE END.

PRINTED BY BALLANTYNE, HANSON AND CO.
EDINBURGH AND LONDON

www.ingramcontent.com/pod-product-compliance
Lightning Source LLC
Chambersburg PA
CBHW020822230426
43666CB00007B/1060